Mike Becker, Becker Helicopters

About this Publication

Document Name:

Principles and Methods of Instruction

Series:

For Helicopter Pilots

Edition:

Second, January 2022

Principal Author:

Mike Becker, ATPL(H), FIR, FER, Diploma (Training and Assessment)

Editor:

Bev Austen, BTech(CompSt), MEd(DTL)

Copyright

Copyright © 2014 Becker Helicopter Services Pty Ltd

Photos and Illustrations

The majority of photos and illustrations in this document have been sourced from Becker Helicopter Services Pty Ltd. The remainder are taken from the internet from various sources; Every effort has been made to ensure images with Creative Commons Licences have been used and appropriate attribution provided.

Disclaimer

Nothing in this text supersedes any operational documents issued by any civil aviation authority or regulatory body, aircraft, engine, and avionics manufacturers, or the operators of aircraft throughout the world. No responsibility is taken for the interpretation and application of the information contained in this document. Managing the safety of the aircraft is the sole responsibility of the pilot-in-command.

Every possible effort has been made to establish the accuracy of the information contained in this book. however, the author, Becker Helicopter Services Pty Ltd, accept no responsibility for errors or omissions.

The Publisher and the Author make no representations or warranties for the accuracy or completeness of the contents of this work and specifically disclaim all warranties, including without limitation warranties of fitness for a particular purpose. No warranty may be created or extended by sales or promotional materials. The advice and strategies contained herein may not be suitable for every situation. This work is sold with the understanding that the author is not engaged in rendering legal, accounting, or other professional services. If professional assistance is required, the services of a competent professional person should be sought. Neither the Publisher nor the Author shall be liable for damages arising therefrom.

The fact that an organisation or website is referred to in this work as a citation and/or a potential source of further information does not mean that the author or the Publisher endorses the information the organisation or website may provide or recommendations it may make. Further, readers should be aware that internet websites listed in this work may have changed or disappeared between when this work was written and when it is read.

Principles and Methods of Instruction *for Helicopter Pilots*

Contents

aAbout this Publication 1
Contents 2
About the Author 5

Australian Regulations 6

PIRC Exam 6
Part 61 Licencing Structure 7
    Licensing Structure Overview 8
    Licence Types 8
    Aircraft Category Ratings 9
    Aircraft Class or Type Ratings 9
    Aircraft Design Feature Endorsements 10
    Operational Ratings 10
Pilot Licence Building 11

The Helicopter Instructor 13

Personal Qualities 14

The Trainee 17

Personality types 18
    Choleric 18
    Phlegmatic 18
    Sanguine 19
    Melancholy 19
    Summary 19
How to deal with problem trainees 20
How to Deal with Experienced Trainee Pilots 22
Summary 22

Division of Responsibilities 23

Fundamentals of Instruction 25

Definition of Learning 25
Characteristics of Learning 26
The Laws of Learning 27
Perception and Insight 28
Motivation 29
Knowledge of Results 30
The Learning Curve 30
Duration and Organisation of Lessons 30
Application of the Skill 31
The Transfer of Learning 32
Habit Formation 32

Psychology of Learning 33

Maslow's Hierarchy of Needs 33
Douglas McGregor's X and Y Theory 34
    Comparing Theory X and Theory Y 35
    Exercise 36
    Summary 36
Fredick Herzberg Two Factor Theory 37

- What do people want from their jobs? ... 37
- Motivation-Hygiene Theory ... 37
- A Simple Diagram ... 38
- Step One: Eliminate Job Dissatisfaction ... 38
- Step Two: Create Conditions for Job Satisfaction ... 39
- Key Points ... 39
- Apply This to Your Life ... 39
- Summary ... 40
- Defence Mechanisms ... 40
- Stress and Anxiety ... 41
- The Instructor's Role in Human Relations ... 41
- Barriers To Effective Communication ... 43

The Teaching Process ... 44
- Effective Communication ... 44
- Phases in the Teaching Process ... 45

Teaching Methods ... 46
- The Lesson ... 46
  - Lesson Introduction ... 46
  - Lesson Development ... 47
  - Aviation Lessons ... 48
- Long Brief ... 48
- Pre-flight Brief ... 50
- Thumbnail Brief ... 52

Use of Lesson Plans ... 53

Question Techniques ... 55
- Effective Questions ... 56
- Questioning Techniques ... 57
- Written Tests ... 58

A Systems Approach to Training ... 59
- Task Analysis ... 59
- Behavioural Objectives ... 59
  - Performance ... 60
  - Standards ... 60
  - Conditions ... 61
- Planning and Conduct of Training ... 61
- Evaluation of Training ... 61
- Competency-based training ... 62
- Summary ... 63

Training Aids ... 64
- Why use Training Aids ... 64
- Types of Training Aids ... 64
  - Projection Equipment ... 64
  - Non-Projection Equipment ... 65
- Managing Training Aids ... 68
- Conclusion ... 69

Appendices ... 70
- Appendix A: PIRC Exam Competencies ... 70

- Appendix B: Example Lesson Plan - Elementary Handling 1 73
  - Briefing And Planning 74
  - Sortie Plan 74
  - Revision And Self Study 76

References 77

Abbreviations 78

About the Author

Mike Becker is one of Australia's most experienced helicopter instructors, with over 16,000 hours of rotary-wing flight experience. His career has taken him from the mountains in New Zealand to the outback of Australia, to the jungles of Papua New Guinea. He has also worked in the United States, Italy and Borneo.

He has flown a range of helicopter types – the Robinson R22, Robinson R44, Bell 47, Hughes 269, Hughes 500, Bell 206, Bell 427, Bell 212, EC120, Dragon Fly, Brantley B2B, Enstrom EF28, Sikorsky S62A, Hiller H12ET, Aerospatial AS350, Agusta 109E Power, Agusta 109S Grand, and the Agusta 119 Koala.

He is experienced in a vast range of helicopter operations including high altitude, remote area operations, mustering, firefighting, tourism, sling load operations, specialised long line operations, search and rescue, and Night Vision Goggles operations.

Mike is a Grade One Flight Instructor and Flight Examiner who holds an Australian Air Transport Pilots Licence (Helicopter) and an Australian Commercial Pilots Licence (Fixed Wing).

Mike is the Chief Pilot and Head of Training for his own business Becker Helicopters in Australia. He, and his wife Jan, established Becker Helicopters in 1997 with one Bell 47 and have grown the business through a love of helicopters, hard work, and determination.

Mike is the recipient of many awards, including the "Captain John Ashton Award for Flight Standards and Aviation Safety" by the Guild of Air Pilots and Air Navigators of London, which was awarded in recognition of over 18,000 accident-free flight training hours at Becker Helicopters. Mike has also authored "Mike Becker's Helicopter Handbook", first published in 1986, along with a range of theory books and instructional videos.

Principles and Methods of Instruction *for Helicopter Pilots*

Australian Regulations

Part 61 of Civil Aviation Safety Regulations 1998[1] prescribes the requirements and standards for the issue of flight crew licences, ratings and other authorisations, including those issued to pilots and flight engineers. It also includes the privileges, limitations, and conditions on such authorisations and rules for logging flight time.

Under Part 61, a pilot must hold a Flight Instructor Rating (FIR) to conduct any flight training.

PIRC Exam

To gain an FIR, the candidate must have completed a Pilot Instructor Rating Common (PIRC) examination after completing either:

- a Principles and Methods of Instruction (PMI) course with an approved helicopter flight school; or
- a Certificate IV in workplace training and assessment; or
- a tertiary qualification of some sort.

The PIRC exam is a generic 50 question 2-hour multi-choice exam. On completing the PIRC, the pilot will also need to attain at least one (1) Training Endorsement (TE) for an FIR to be issued.

Reference

CASA Pilot Instructor Rating Common Examination (PIRC) web page[2]

Tip: Try searching the internet for practice PIRC cyber exams.

Reference materials

This book has been prepared as a training reference for the PMI course to align with Australian regulations. In addition, the Civil Aviation Safety Authority of Australia (CASA) has compiled a list of references materials they have used to construct the exam.

CASA has identified the **Aviation Instructor's Handbook** *(FAA-H-8083-9)*[3] as the primary reference text for the PIRC examination.

Theories of motivation

A candidate is required to have a high-level understanding of the following theories of motivation:

- Hierarchy of Needs by Abraham Maslow
- X and Y theory by Douglas McGregor, and
- Two Factor theory by Frederick Herzberg.

To find out more about these theories of motivation, CASA recommends the following optional references:

- **Human Factors in Flight** by Frank Hawkins or any human factors book on 'memory', 'motivation', 'stress', etc.
- **Preparing Instructional Objectives** by Robert F Mager for more information on behavioural objectives.
- **Measuring Instructional Results** by Robert F Mager for more information on behavioural objectives.

---

[1] https://www.casa.gov.au/content-search/rules/part-61-casr-flight-crew-licensing

[2] https://www.casa.gov.au/standard-page/pilot-instructor-rating-common-examination-pirc

[3] https://www.faa.gov/regulations_policies/handbooks_manuals/aviation/aviation_instructors_handbook/

Part 61 Licencing Structure

Once the candidate has completed an approved Principles and Methods of Instruction (PMI) course and has completed the PIRC exam, the candidate must:

- complete training relevant to the Training Endorsement (TE) applied for, and then
- conduct a Proficiency Test for at least one TE to attach to the Flight Instructor Rating (FIR).

Historical qualification structure

Historically, a helicopter instructor was required to do an entire 40-hour instructor course to become a Grade 2 Instructor to deliver training towards a licence. Under CAR 5 (before the introduction of Part 61), once qualified as a flight instructor, the instructor could also deliver training for any other rating or endorsement in which the instructor was qualified, including low level, sling, type ratings, NVFR and IFR.

Part 61 Flight Instructor Rating with TEs attached

With the introduction of Part 61, a pilot now requires a TE attached to the FIR. To deliver training towards a licence, a flight instructor requires either a Grade 3, 2 or 1 TE.

Non-Licence training: other TEs

Under Part 61, a flight instructor must hold a TE to conduct related flight training. For example, for a flight instructor to conduct Night VFR flight training they must hold either a Night VFR TE or Instrument Flight TE. A flight instructor does not require a Grade 3, 2 or 1 TE as these endorsements are only required to conduct flight training towards a licence.

FIR training course

The FIR establishes the foundation theory of instruction, while the TEs establish the flight instruction techniques specific to the TE. As a result, flight training towards an FIR is tailored to the TEs required by the flight instructor.

Advantages of Part 61

The advantage of Part 61 licencing structure is that individual pilots can do the minimum training required to gain the relevant TEs applicable to their area of expertise. They do not have to do a full 40-hour course if there is no intention to teach new pilots towards the issue of a licence.

Privileges and limitations

Just what a Flight Instructor can do and the limitations on what can be done will significantly vary depending on what type of TE/s the Flight Instructor holds.

Reference to Part 61 and the Manual of Standards (MOS) is essential to understand the privileges and limitations specific to each Flight Instructor's qualifications.

Principles and Methods of Instruction *for Helicopter Pilots*

Licensing Structure Overview

The following provides an overview of the Part 61 licencing structure.

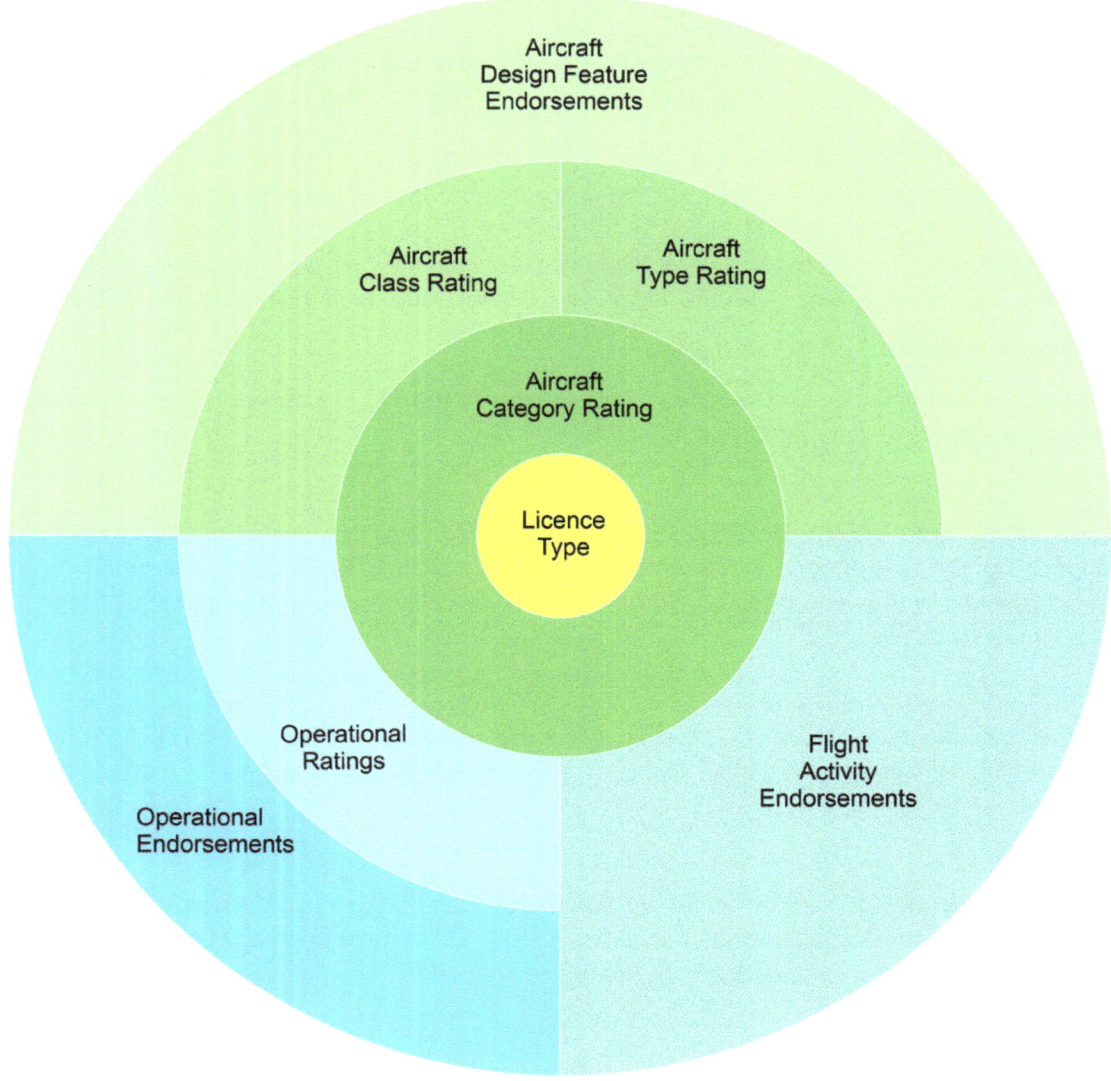

> **Reference**
>
> The *Part 61 Manual of Standards Instrument 2014*[4] details the requirements for each of the ratings and endorsements.

Licence Types

Classification	Code	Description
Powered Aircraft	RPL	Recreational Pilot Licence
	PPL	Private Pilot Licence
	CPL	Commercial Pilot Licence
	MPL	Multi-Crew Pilot Licence
	ATPL	Air Transport Pilot Licence
Gliders	GPL	Glider Pilot Licence
Balloons		Balloon Licence (not covered by Part 61)

---

[4] https://www.legislation.gov.au/Details/F2021C00449/Html/Volume_1

Aircraft Category Ratings

Every licence issued is assigned to a specific aircraft category. For example, Commercial Pilot Licence (Helicopter) or CPL(H).

Code	Description
A	Aeroplane
H	Helicopter
P	Powered-lift aircraft
G	Gyroplane
AS	Airship

Aircraft Class or Type Ratings

Every aircraft is assigned to either a class or a type. When a pilot holds a class rating, the pilot is authorised to fly all aircraft in that class subject to completing a flight review in that aircraft type.

Category	Code	Class description
Aeroplane	SEA	Single-engine aeroplane
	MEA	Multi-engine aeroplane
	[TYP]	Type rating aeroplane with a specific designator
Helicopter	SEH	Single-engine helicopter
	[TYP]	Type rating helicopter with a specific designator
Gyroplane	SEG	Single-engine gyroplane
Airship	ASP	Airship

Reference

CASA website: Aircraft ratings explained[5]

Prescription of Aircraft and Ratings — CASR Part 61 (Edition 8) Instrument 2021[6]

---

[5] https://www.casa.gov.au/licences-and-certificates/pilots/ratings-reviews-and-endorsements/ratings-and-endorsements/aircraft-ratings-explained

[6] https://www.legislation.gov.au/Details/F2021L00622

Aircraft Design Feature Endorsements

Aircraft with unique design features also require a pilot to hold the associated design feature endorsement.

Code	Design feature endorsements
TWU	Tail wheel Undercarriage
RU	Retractable Undercarriage
SKIL	Ski Landing Gear
MPPC	Manual Propeller Pitch Control (piston engine only)
GTE	Gas Turbine Engine
MEAC	Multi Engine Centerline Thrust
PXS	Pressurisation System
FLP	Floatplane
FLH	Floating Hull
GLAG	Float Alighting Gear

Operational Ratings

Operational ratings combined with at least one endorsement provide the authority to conduct different types of operations.

Code	Operational Rating	Description
IR	Instrument rating	Any flight operation under IFR as well as a flight operation at night under VFR (other than NVIS or aerial application operations)
PIFR	Private instrument rating	A single-pilot operation under IFR in a private operation
NVFR	Night VFR rating	A flight operation at night under VFR (other than NVIS or aerial application operations)
NVIS	Night vision rating	A flight operation at night under VFR using NVIS
LL	Low-level rating	A low-level flight operation
AA	Aerial application rating	An aerial application flight operation below 500 feet AGL
FIR	Flight instructor rating	Flight training for pilot licences, ratings and endorsements. Conduct flight reviews. Type variant differences training and training for general competency in an aircraft class or type.
FER	Flight examiner rating	To conduct flight tests and proficiency checks. To grant ratings and endorsements.
SIR	Simulator instructor rating	To conduct flight training in a flight simulation training device.

Instrument Rating Endorsements

The Instrument Rating includes the following endorsements.

Code	Instrument Rating Endorsements
SEA	Single-Engine Aeroplane
MEA	Multi-Engine Aeroplane
SEH	Single Engine Helicopter
MEH	Multi-Engine Helicopter
IAP2D	Instrument Approach 2 dimensional
IAP3D	Instrument Approach 3 dimensional
PL	Powered-lift (Reserved)
G	Gyroplane (Reserved)
AS	Airship (Reserved)

Pilot Licence Building

Think of your licence as a building. The rooms represent different classes, types, ratings or endorsements. As a pilot obtains additional ratings and endorsements, the building grows, more rooms are opened up, and more floors are added.

The diagram below illustrates a building for a pilot who has a Single Engine Helicopter Class, with Gas Turbine Engine Design Feature, as well as the Operational Ratings Low Level, Aerial Application and NVFR. Where an operational rating is obtained, this may lead to additional floors with more endorsements available.

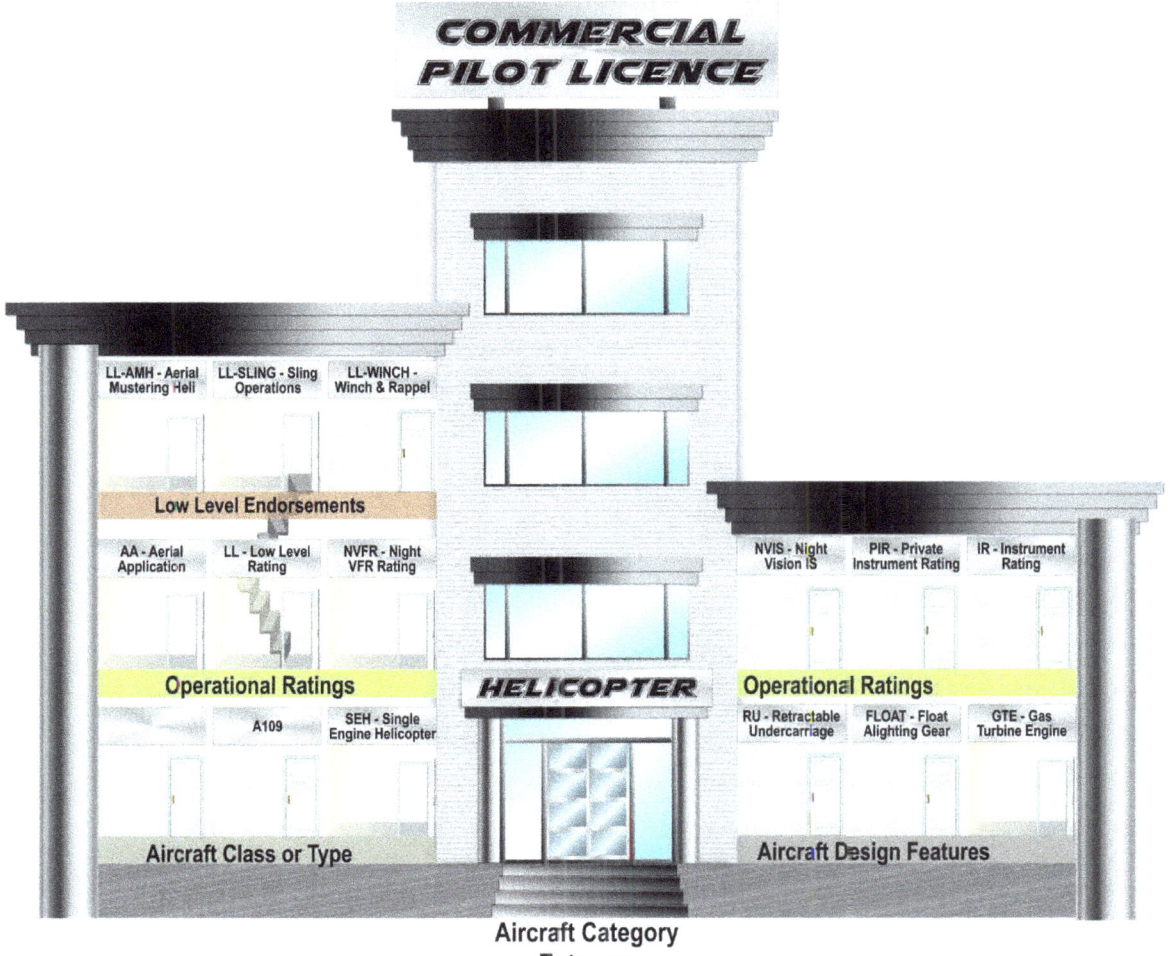

Principles and Methods of Instruction *for Helicopter Pilots*

Example 2:

In this example, we show an experienced Flight Instructor and Flight Examiner. As you can see, this pilot has more ratings, which has opened up more floors and rooms in his licence building. The Instructor and Examiner ratings are represented as a "lift", which has access to all the other floors (other ratings and endorsements).

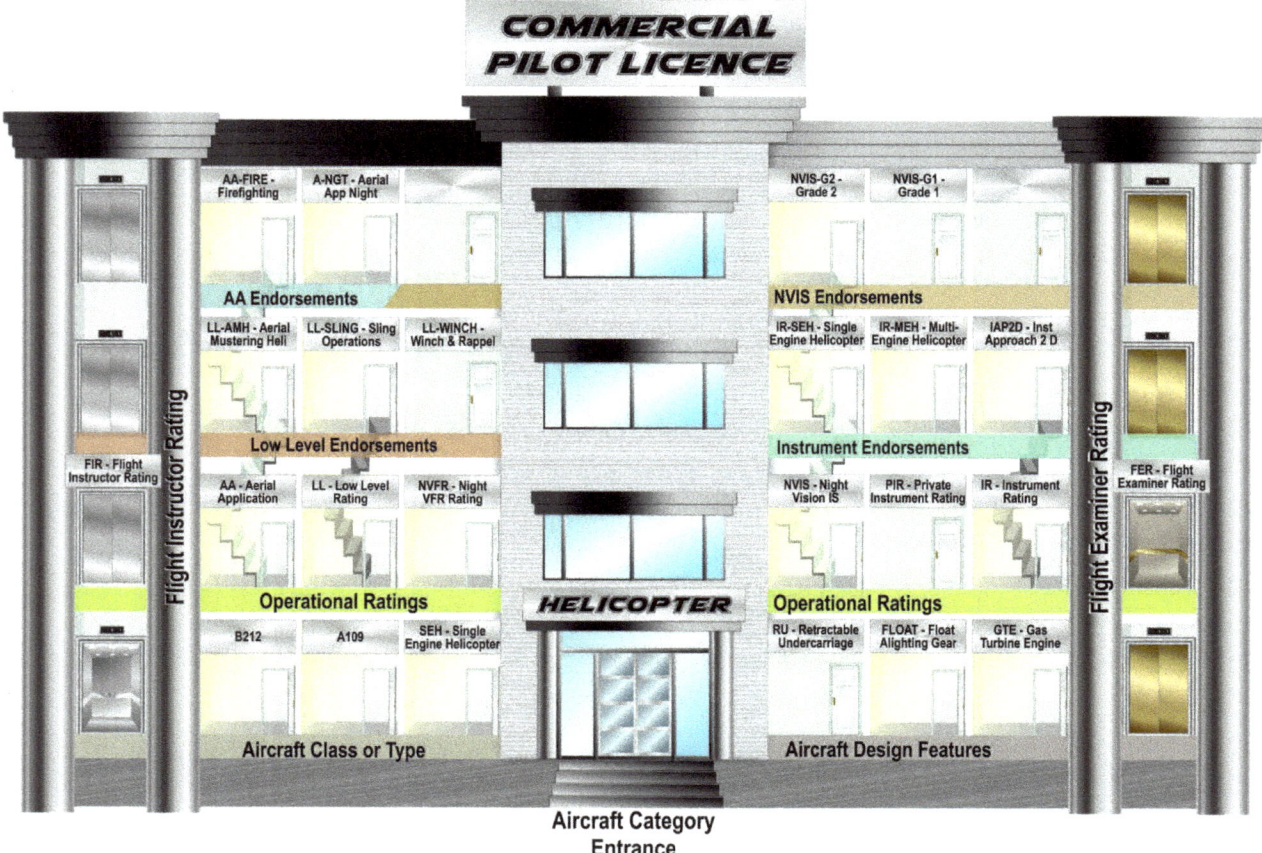

The Helicopter Instructor

> **Recommended Reading:**
>
> Aviation Instructor's Handbook: *Chapter 8 – Aviation Instructor Responsibilities and Professionalism*[7]

Who became instructors in the past

Few pilots who become instructors are initially motivated to flight training as an ultimate career, many regard flight training as either a step to help build hours on a career path leading to employment in something bigger and supposedly better or on the flip side as a retirement job having gained many thousands of hours in their area of the industry and now want something a bit more stable, keeping them at home at night.

All pilots giving instruction in the future

Under Part 61 all pilots giving instruction will have to be Flight Instructors so a pilot may only be gaining the PMI portion of the Flight Instructors course so that they can conduct check and training, conduct mustering training, give sling load or firefighting training or other operational training. The pilot may not be interested in becoming an instructor to train pilots to gain a licence but instead, use it as a tool to allow them to conduct their job within an organisation as they have been doing in the past. This is a fundamental shift in the philosophy of the regulator (CASA).

Professional development

Flight training is an excellent way to increase and consolidate your skill levels, professional knowledge and experience. It allows you to do things in a helicopter you would not normally do and, therefore, gives you a much better appreciation of the helicopter's limits and yours.

Professional responsibility

Your primary professional responsibility is to ensure that your trainees develop skills, knowledge, confidence, and most importantly the right attitudes and behaviours needed to fly safely. This is a heavy responsibility and one which the regulator (CASA) by legislation will be holding you to.

Instructing requires hard work and total commitment. If you are not prepared to accept this responsibility and hard work, then you should not be looking at instructing as a career option.

Measures of success

Different pilots can measure success as a flying instructor in different ways.

- You may regard yourself as successful if you get a full-time job as an instructor.
- Your employer, who is operating a commercial enterprise with the expectation of making a profit, may measure your success by your productivity and your ability to make a profit in excess of what you cost.
- CASA will regard you as successful if your trainees consistently meet and maintain the CASA pilot licence standards and pass flight tests.
- Your trainees will regard you as successful if your instruction is perceived as professional, effective, gives them good value for money and they are passing their exams and tests.

Ultimately your success is measured in your attitude and ability to do what you are doing and the attitude and ability of your trainees.

This flying instructors PMI course is designed to further develop your attitude and ability to meet this aim

---

[7] https://www.faa.gov/regulations_policies/handbooks_manuals/aviation/aviation_instructors_handbook/media/10_aih_chapter_8.pdf

Adapting techniques

Although flying training is based on teaching principles, which remain relatively constant, it is also an art form in which different techniques are perfectly acceptable and which can change with time to reflect the changes in the operating environment. True professional pilots, like good artists, have an open mind with a desire to continually learn from other professionals. During the course you will find these differences in technique among staff instructors, reflecting their individual experience as a pilot. Although standardisation of procedures is desirable to prevent confusion, absolute standardisation of techniques among professionals is almost impossible to achieve and inhibits new ideas.

When exposed to differences in flying techniques you (and in turn your trainees) must never be reluctant to ask why. Every procedure and technique, which is used and taught, must be capable of logical explanation. If it is not, the procedure or technique is probably incorrect, inappropriate or not truly understood.

Personal Qualities

A helicopter instructor needs to develop and possess certain personal qualities.

Sincerity

This quality implies frankness, honesty and integrity. Instructors must be able to admit their own mistakes and inadequacies if they are to be respected by their trainees and fellow instructors.

Tolerance

Instructors must be prepared to accept other people, particularly their trainees, as they are, warts and all, and adapt themselves to work with their different personalities.

There is no place for racial, religious, sexual or other discrimination when working as an instructor. (Excluding discrimination to trainees who do not like rugby union)

Personal appearance and habits

(Chetan, 2019)

These qualities have a significant effect on an instructor's professional image and employability. Employers and trainees expect instructors to look and act like professionals. First impressions are lasting. Punctuality and reliability are important as is wearing deodorant, and not eating garlic the night before.

Turning up for work late, with a hangover, smelling of alcohol might put you in the category of a legend but it will not see you employed for very long or have the respect of your trainees.

If you have long hair, have it tied up and neat, nose rings and other extreme personal habits do not bode well for trainee confidence in their instructor in the beginning.

Demeanour

This means your personality should not be offensive. Instructors should avoid extremes of demeanour such as anger, flippancy, and sarcasm. You should be reasonable in your demands on trainees and should try to display a calm and pleasant demeanour even when frustrated or provoked. Offending a trainee for the sake of proving you are better is another good way to become unemployable. Understanding your personality type and the trainees' personality type will assist in this area (covered later).

Proper language

The use of profane or obscene language is objectionable to many people. Instructors should also be careful not to use too much professional language or abbreviations too early on in the course. The trainee must understand precisely what you are saying and more importantly what you mean.

Skill

You must demonstrate a high level of skill and accuracy. Besides giving demonstrations skillfully and convincingly you must remember that trainees learn quickly by example and will imitate bad habits as well as good ones.

Knowledge

To explain a subject clearly, it is necessary to know more about it than must be taught.

You should keep yourself well informed on all subjects related to the flying training arena.

In addition, the trainee is looking forward to a career in the helicopter industry and the instructor should be able to foster confidence and respect by being able to express intelligent views on current trends in equipment development, operational techniques and CASA changes.

Professionalism (Discipline)

The trainee looks to the instructor on the ground and in the air for an example of what a professional pilot should be. The relationship between the trainee and instructor should be an easy one in which problems of any kind are freely aired. There should be an atmosphere of friendly authority that discourages frivolity but allows frank discussion.

Patience

A trainee learns at his or her own pace and even when doing their best forgets a great deal of what is being taught. Many points are driven home only after constant practice, repetition and rehearsal. Failure to grasp them readily should never cause displays of impatience, frustration, anger or ridicule by the instructor. Such outbursts usually only result in trainee/instructor anxiety, bewilderment and mutiny!

The instructor should instead assume that the wrong method or approach to the problem is being used and try a different angle. Not all trainees learn the same.

Restraint

There are always times when a trainee seems to be especially slow to learn or lacks some quality that upsets the instructor. This can prove to be destructive to the relationship, however, it must be remembered that no purpose will be served in giving way to anger in the form of an unleashed outburst. If reproach is necessary (and at times it is) then it is most effectively delivered in a restrained and reasoned manner.

Understanding

The instructor must understand that the trainee also has a life outside of flying with personal and financial problems that can reflect on the trainee's performance or lack thereof.

(RODNAE Productions, 2020)

The trainee's confidence can be completely undermined by brooding on some difficulty, which might easily be solved after a little sound advice. The instructor must often be something of a psychologist, counsellor, and accountant. Often just showing interest over a cup of coffee is enough.

Personality

No one likes a boring monotonous lecture, where everything is covered and done by the "numbers" but where the trainee quickly switches off and thinks of other more interesting things.

Everyone has a distinct personality, and this should be used to inject some fun and excitement into what is being taught. Brief (emphasis on brief and relevant) digressions and touches of humour do much to relieve the strain and tension on some of the more demanding exercises and will encourage the trainee with renewed effort and enthusiasm.

The pursuit of excellence

Flying instructors, like true professionals, are never satisfied with their standards of skill and knowledge. They are committed to continual self-improvement through practice, repetition, rehearsal, research and discussion. Trainees will usually emulate this personal quality and attitude to their lasting benefit.

The Trainee

> **Recommended Reading:**
>
> Aviation Instructor's Handbook: Chapter 2 - Human Behaviour [8]
>
> Personality Plus by Florence Littauer

All trainees come to the flight school after making a personal decision to learn to fly or upgrade or add to their skills or simply to conduct currency training or a proficiency check.

This decision has not come lightly; often it has taken a period of thought and discussions with the Flight School. It means they are going to outlay a significant amount of money (often everything they have) and in most cases are travelling from a distant place to live for a period of time.

They will constantly need reassurance and support. Anything negative is usually multiplied by a factor of 10 and anything positive only lasts in their memory till the following evening.

They come from different countries, cultures, religious backgrounds, and circumstances.

They will also have their personality which you must be able to understand and use to assist in the teaching process. Understanding these personalities will allow you to better understand them and modify your approach to get a better result earlier on in their training.

---

[8] https://www.faa.gov/regulations_policies/handbooks_manuals/aviation/aviation_instructors_handbook/media/04_aih_chapter_2.pdf

Personality types

> **Recommended Activity:**
>
> Prior to commencing this section complete the Personality Profile in Florence Littauer's book ***Personality Plus***

Choleric

The powerful choleric personality is the person who wants to get things moving. A choleric is a dynamic person who dreams the impossible dream and is always striving to achieve.

The choleric is one of the easiest types of personalities to get along with as long as you live by his golden rule, that is

"Do it my way NOW!!!"

Some choleric personality traits include:

- Born leader
- Compulsive need for change
- Strong-willed and decisive
- Can run anything
- Goal orientated
- Organises well
- Delegates work
- Thrives on opposition
- Has little need for friends
- Is usually right (just ask him/her)
- Excels in emergencies

George W Bush
(Draper, 2003)

Gough Whitlam
(NAA, n.d.-a)

Phlegmatic

The peaceful phlegmatic personality is the person who is the buffer for the emotions of all the other personality types. A phlegmatic is relaxed and calm, the world could be on fire and everything falling down around them and they will sit back and watch. Nothing seems to bother them and they like nothing more than to watch the world go by.

Some phlegmatic personality traits include:

- Low key personality, easy-going
- Cool calm and collected
- Patient and well balanced
- Happily reconciled to life
- Has administrative ability
- Mediates problems
- Easy to get along with
- Has many friends
- Is a good listener

Barrack Obama
(Souza, 2012)

John Howard
(Portrait of PM John Winston Howard, Circa 2001, 2006)

Sanguine

The popular fun-loving sanguine personality is the out there turning work into fun. Looking for the fairy tale, they are emotional and demonstrative. They love being around people, are optimistic and outgoing. They can be very talkative.

Some sanguine personality traits include:

- Appealing personality
- Talkative and a storyteller
- Life of the party
- Memory for colour
- Holds onto the listener
- Good on stage
- Wide-eyed and innocent
- Enthusiastic and expressive
- Curious
- Always a child
- Volunteers for jobs
- Creative and colourful
- Inspires and charms others
- Makes friends easily
- Seems exciting

Bill Clinton
(McNeely, 1993)

Bob Hawke
(Portrait of PM Robert James Lee Hawke, Date Unknown., 2005)

Melancholy

The perfect melancholy personality is the person who just wants to get things organised and lined up straight. They think deeply, like to follow schedules and responds best to having and following a laid out plan.

Some melancholy personality traits include:

- Deep, thoughtful and analytical
- Serious and purposeful
- Genius intellect
- Talented and creative
- Likes lists, charts, graphs and figures
- Detail conscious
- Orderly and organised
- Neat and tidy
- A perfectionist with high standards
- Economical
- Deep concern and compassion
- Seeks ideal mate

Abraham Lincoln
(Public Domain)

Kevin Rudd
(NAA, n.d.-b)

Summary

If you can understand yourself, and you can understand your trainee, you can then start to create an environment that each trainee can relate to and appreciate, making you the "Best" instructor they have ever had. Play to each personality and give them what they "need" to learn.

For example:

- A choleric trainee needs relevant information, the how and why and they need it all now
- A sanguine trainee needs to hear a joke and have fun learning
- A melancholy wants to see the schedule and see that you are following a plan, and
- A phlegmatic trainee will just go with whatever way you want to teach it.

Principles and Methods of Instruction *for Helicopter Pilots*

How to deal with problem trainees

Over confidence

A conceited trainee often displays a degree of confidence, which is not borne out by their ability. The instructor should insist on a high standard of accuracy and airmanship, don't let them cut corners; try to slow them down. Pull them up on all inaccuracies in a firm but fair manner, so that the trainee is aware of their shortcomings. Ignore their expected grumbling.

A more difficult case occasionally arises in which a feeling of inferiority or insecurity is cloaked in an attitude of aggressiveness. The trainee may display nervous gestures or mannerisms, doing what we often call *"the funky chicken"* where they do something completely out of the blue and opposite to what is expected.

This problem requires careful handling since repressing the apparent over-confidence may only aggravate the problem.

Under confidence

The nervous, timid trainee needs encouragement. They tend to be extremely self-critical and become discouraged if not assured that their progress is "normal".

They should be praised freely when doing well and mistakes should be carefully explained without undue reflection on their ability (or lack thereof).

Care must be taken in the air to avoid any signs of apprehension while in control of the helicopter.

Forgetfulness

Most trainees forget a lot of what they are taught and facts must be ingrained by constant revision. The use of checklists and making the trainee say the checks out loud every time reinforces the correct technique.

Carelessness or neglect warrants a good direct conversation, pointing out the forgetfulness but also arming them with tools to fix the problem (checklists, saying the checks out loud).

Sometimes genuinely poor memory is encountered. Forgetful trainees should be made to take a very active part during dual instruction and should be called upon to recount on the ground what they have learned in the air.

Inconsistency

The process of learning is an irregular one and instructors are sometimes discouraged when they find their trainees becoming stale from time to time. This is because the mind can become saturated with new ideas and the trainee's receptivity often deteriorates until the fresh information has been consolidated in the memory. Flying training takes place in an entirely new medium and it is not uncommon for a trainee to make a slow start, only to progress rapidly at a later stage when they feel more at home. It is, therefore, unwise to worry unduly if the trainee appears to stand still for a while. When this does occur, it is best to either revise earlier lessons until the trainee recovers their pace or even move on to something completely different or sometimes even more challenging. This change in itself is sometimes enough for the trainee to get back on track.

A lengthy lapse, however, is usually due to some more profound difficulty and requires closer investigation.

Apathy

If a trainee becomes unusually slow, inattentive, or erratic, it can be due to several troubles. It may, of course, be mere backsliding but it would be wrong to assume this without first having investigated the case. It is always possible that the trainee may be distracted by some problem of his or her own which the instructor should try to uncover.

The most common reasons for a loss of enthusiasm are:

- Private worries
- Broken instructor/trainee relations, or
- Uncertain if flying helicopters is for them.

Private worries

Domestic and financial stresses can be distracting, and the trainee is usually reluctant to discuss them, particularly if it involves a topic with a lot of emotion attached to it.

Before approaching the trainee, do some research, ask some of his or her close friends, other trainees, parents, or spouse to see if you can find a reason for the worries before having a discussion. Sometimes the trainee should have a break and sort the problems out before continuing.

Other problems include peer pressure, where the trainee is not progressing at the same rate as the other trainees and will find reasons to disguise this.

Broken instructor/trainee relations

Often personalities clash especially when you get a strong, older trainee being taught by a young, nervous instructor. Another common reason for this is when a trainee has flown with a senior instructor then ends up flying with a junior instructor, they don't think they are getting the same value for money. This is another reason to have a standard form of training so that the trainee does not feel there is a great difference between instructors.

Most times the problem sorts itself out, in extreme cases, a change of instructor will be required.

Uncertain if flying helicopters is for them

This may come about because the trainee is afraid the helicopter is going to kill them!!! Lack of confidence in the helicopter, often brought about by the instructor complaining about flying a "shit box" or how this helicopter keeps "breaking down" does nothing but encourage this perception. It is very important for the instructor to ooze confidence, and if the helicopter has a snag of some sort, to treat it as if this will happen because after all, the helicopter is only a piece of machinery and machinery will wear out. This is the process to get it fixed. Any complaints about helicopters should be directed at the CFI or Chief Pilot, not the trainee.

Others often wonder if they are making the right career choice, often a talk over a cup of coffee will answer that question.

Other causes may be a past bad experience, a phobia of some sort, or just bad advice from a third party.

Negativity multiplies

When two or more people get together it is common for them to complain. If there is a fault with an instructor or a school, that negative comment will multiply by a factor of 10. In this case, it is easy for the trainees, once they have started down the path of doom and gloom, to blow everything out of proportion. It is important to deal with this as soon as possible by confronting the trainees involved. Ask them some simple questions, find the source of the problem, make assurances and if necessary, change your procedures.

How to Deal with Experienced Trainee Pilots

As instructors, we will also have to deal with very experienced pilots who are at the school to up-skill, conduct some currency training or who need a proficiency check for a particular rating. This can lead to a unique set of issues around each individual's paradigm and expectations over and above the usual trainee issues stated above.

Based on their experience the instructor and the pilot receiving the training should have some professional courtesy towards each other realising that each has a role to play in the training and assessing cycle.

Setting out a plan and then agreeing on the ground rules before the flight is very important as there have been many accidents where each senior pilot thought the other was in control. This includes agreeing on a hand-over and takeover procedure and discussing techniques.

Before commencing any training or checking it is best to sit down and work a plan that is put in writing. This can be as simple as verbally agreeing, all the way to a formal written training plan. This way both the instructor and the trainee know what to expect. Recognition of prior learning, interpretation of any current regulation, cross-referencing with CASA for clarification and agreement on payment can all be done before the actual lessons.

The instructor must assert their authority as the leader in this scenario and guide and mentor the other pilot who has come to receive the training.

Summary

The trainees can be summarised by looking at their personality types. Often a certain personality type will lead to that trainee displaying a typical problem. The more experience you gain, the more you will see history repeat itself, remember don't take their problems as necessarily a fault of you, instead be a good 'teacher' and guide them with empathy through the training.

Mike Becker, Becker Helicopters

Division of Responsibilities

As an instructor, you will have responsibilities to different people and organisations.

At times these responsibilities may create a situation where your loyalties are divided, solving these problems requires common sense, sound judgement and a strong belief in professional ethics.

CASA

Instructors receive their legal authority to practice their profession from CASA and they are responsible to the CASA to maintain their professional competence and to observe and teach CASA rules and procedures.

Although this at times can be difficult, as CASA is constantly changing the rules and regulations, and different CASA employees tend to interpret the rules differently.

The best way around this is to rely on the mentoring of the head of the Flight School you are working for and run with the interpretation they operate under.

Your employer

As a licensed instructor, you can only teach within the approvals you have. In most cases, this means operating through an approved Flight School or approved check and training organisation. There is little that can be done outside of either a Part 141, 142 or CAR 217 organisation. Your employer is giving you the opportunity to practice your profession and gain income. You have a responsibility to be loyal to the company, perform professionally and personally so that trainees will be attracted to and continue with your employer's organisation.

Your employer has a responsibility to operate within the CASA rules and regulations and within any exemptions they may also have in place. This can be a changing minefield so help your employer by trying to remain abreast of current regulation and bring any anomalies to their attention.

CASA will have approved a Company Operations Manual so this is the document that you can rely on to serve the interests of both CASA and your employer at the same time.

Your trainees

Your trainees are always putting their trust and their lives (and those of their future passengers/trainees) in your hands. Often your trainees are paying money for your services. This commitment of money, time and personal safety demand your best efforts in return. Flying is an expensive activity and you have a responsibility to plan and conduct a training program, which will give your trainees the best outcome.

Principles and Methods of Instruction *for Helicopter Pilots*

Yourself

Ultimately you have a responsibility to yourself to maintain your safety and ethics towards what you are doing. If in doubt, ask questions. As a professional, it is up to you to maintain your knowledge, skills and behaviours in your profession.

Mike Becker, Becker Helicopters

Fundamentals of Instruction

As a teacher, a flying instructor must first understand the theory of learning before learning the theory and practice of teaching!

The theory of learning has been developed over centuries, and like many theories about human behaviour, it is subject to endless research, some controversy and a great deal of professional jargon. However, the essential elements of the theory are easy to understand and, if applied, will greatly improve the instructor's effectiveness.

> **Recommended Reading:**
> Aviation Instructor's Handbook: *Chapter 3 The Learning Process*[9]

Definition of Learning

Learning is a continuous process throughout life. As a result of learning, a person's way of thinking, feeling and doing may change. In short, a person's behaviour changes.

This observation leads to the following accepted definition of learning.

"Learning is a change in behaviour as a result of experience"

---

[9] https://www.faa.gov/regulations_policies/handbooks_manuals/aviation/aviation_instructors_handbook/media/05_aih_chapter_3.pdf

Characteristics of Learning

Researchers into the learning process generally agree that learning has four characteristics:

- Learning is **purposeful** – trainees must have some purpose or objective
- Learning is a **result of experience** – trainee learns as a result of individual experience
- Learning is **multi-faceted** – learning is rarely limited to a particular lesson
- Learning is an **active process** – effective learning requires trainee participation.

Learning is Purposeful

For learning to occur, a trainee must have some purpose or objective. This may be very specific, such as a desire to apply the knowledge or skill, which is learned as a means to gain some tangible reward. The purpose may also be general to indefinite, such as a desire to improve general knowledge or to occupy idle time. However, a trainee who is deeply committed to a purpose for learning will progress rapidly.

Learning is a Result of Experience

This characteristic follows from the definition of learning. A person can only learn as a result of individual experience.

Learning is Multi-faceted

This simply means that learning is rarely limited to the subject of a particular lesson. In addition to acquiring specific skills, knowledge and behaviours, a trainee will also learn concepts or skills, which may only be indirectly related to a lesson subject. For example, a trainee may learn about the personal philosophies and prejudices of a teacher or fellow trainee or learn some aspect of a skill such as how (or how not!) to use training aids.

Learning is an Active Process

Trainees do not soak up knowledge like a sponge. Effective learning requires a trainee's participation in the learning process.

The Laws of Learning

Education psychologists have evolved some generally accepted laws of learning, which reflect the characteristics already covered. These "Laws" are not just abstract theory; if their meaning is understood and applied, they will improve an instructor's effectiveness:

- The Law of Readiness
- The Law of Exercise
- The Law of Effect
- The Law of Primacy
- The Law of Intensity
- The Law of Recency

The Law of Readiness

The Trainee will learn when they are ready to learn, that is when they perceive some purpose in gaining a particular skill, knowledge or attitude. An instructor can reinforce, or even create, this readiness by making his teaching relevant to a particular skill, knowledge or attitude.

The Law of Exercise

This means that if a skill or knowledge is "exercised", that is, repeated often enough, learning is greatly assisted. To apply this law, an instructor must provide every opportunity for trainees to practice what they have learned while ensuring that the practice is relevant to a specified skill, knowledge or attitude.

The Law of Effect

This law is related to the emotional reaction of a trainee. The emotional effect that a learning experience has on a trainee is important in effective learning. Instructors must always try to create a learning environment that will produce a feeling of satisfaction and achievement, not frustration, fear, anger or confusion. This requires a cautious and thoughtful approach to instruction and lesson planning, of setting immediate objectives which are within a trainee's capabilities, but which present a challenge.

The Law of Primacy

Trainees tend to remember best what they learned first. Basic skills or knowledge should be learned first, as the essential foundations for more complex procedures or techniques later on. This law is reflected in the arrangement of the sequences listed in a syllabus of training. Instructors must also ensure that what is said or done at the beginning of a training session is correct, and trainees must not be allowed to practice incorrect techniques or procedures. "Unlearning" is far more difficult than learning.

The Law of Intensity

Dramatic or exciting experiences are more effective in learning than experience which is boring or routine, provided the intensity of the experience does not create fear or anxiety. This law can be used to good effect by an instructor who uses imagination in lesson planning to create realism and vividness.

The Law of Recency

This law is related to the law of primacy and simply means that a trainee is most likely to remember the last thing learned, provided there is not too much time between training sessions, or between theory and application. Trainees should be encouraged to attend training sessions as frequently as possible. This law can also be applied by summarising at the end of a training session. This is often done by reviewing the lesson objectives and allows for clear and concise emphasising of basic principles and key points delivered from which a trainee can deduce answers to more complex problems which may have been covered in a lesson.

Principles and Methods of Instruction *for Helicopter Pilots*

Perception and Insight

Perception is an essential element in learning; it is what the brain "sees" as a result of inputs from the physical senses, that is, sight, hearing, touch, smell and taste.

Experiments have shown that in the "average" person, the contribution which each of the senses makes to perception is

Sense	Percentage of perception	Image
Sight	75%	
Hearing	13%	
Touch	6%	
Smell	3%	
Taste	3%	

This analysis is the basis of the saying that "a picture is worth a thousand words". Therefore, to ensure clear, accurate and rapid perception, an instructor should involve as many trainees' senses as possible, but in particular sight and hearing.

Insight occurs when the brain links several perceptions to produce understanding and comprehension. Producing insight is an instructor's main responsibility, and depends largely on the quality of the perception achieved. In turn, these depend on the quality of the words and visual images used in the learning process.

Insight will occur without instruction through a process of trial and error. However, this process is, at best, inefficient and, at worst, dangerous (particularly in flying). The instructor must produce an environment in which insight will occur as a result of planned learning, removing the temptation for a trainee to gain insight from trial and error.

Motivation

Motivation is a dominant force governing a trainee's progress. Motivation can be very obvious or it may be difficult to identify. It is usually self-generated by the trainee but can (and should) be re-enforced by the instructor. Motivation can either be positive or negative, the "carrot" or the "stick".

Negative Motivation	Positive Motivation
Negative motivations are those which produce fear or a sense of threat. Although negative motivation can have a purpose in learning, as in the case of an over-confident trainee ("if you do that again I'll ground you!"), it is rarely as effective as positive motivation.	Positive motivation is produced by the promise or achievement of rewards. These may be tangible, like the achievement of financial gain, or intangible, for example, self-satisfaction or social approval. Whatever their nature, positive motivation must be present in all learning experiences. The rewards of learning must be constantly reiterated, the "carrot" must be kept in sight.

Knowledge of Results

In the learning of simple skills, trainees can easily see their own mistakes and correct them. As skills become more complex, trainees need expert advice on their progress and advice on how to fix the mistake if proficiency is to improve.

Positive reinforcement when they are right is just as important as positive correcting advice when they are wrong. Errors should be corrected early; trainees should never be allowed to continue practising mistakes thinking this is normal.

The Learning Curve

Progress in the acquisition of a skill is never a steady, straight-line process. The normal pattern is for early rapid progress, followed by a period of little or no improvement before the learning rate accelerates again. This pattern may be repeated several times during the learning process depending on the complexity of the skill. The period of slow or little progress is called a "plateau of learning", and may occur at different stages in the learning process with different trainees, and are largely unpredictable. The cause of these "plateaus" may be due to many factors, for example, a loss of interest, or the need to consolidate what has been learned very rapidly. Whatever the reason, trainees should be forewarned that these "plateaus" will occur but that progress will return. Unless trainees are prepared, they will become frustrated, under-confident and may lose their desire to learn.

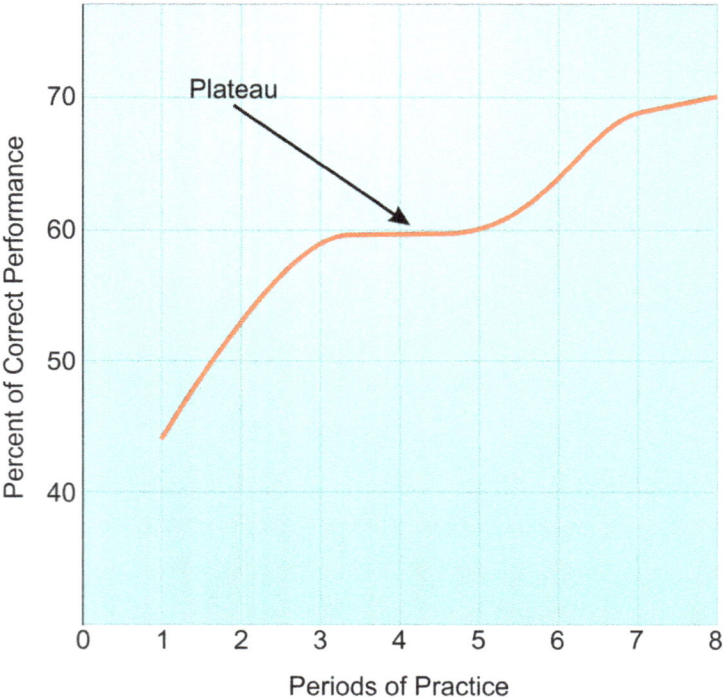

Duration and Organisation of Lessons

In planning for trainee progress, a primary consideration is the time to be spent in practice. At some point, additional practice becomes unproductive. When this point is reached, errors increase and motivation declines. Lessons must be carefully planned to provide the best balance between instructor explanation and demonstration, and trainee practice. This balance will depend upon the complexity of the skill being learned.

Critique versus Evaluation. Trainees need more than a simple evaluation of their performance, that is, whether their performance is right or wrong. Effective learning requires a careful analysis by the instructor of the trainee performance. This analysis becomes the basis of a **critique**, which is a clear explanation of why performance is wrong, and how to correct the problem. This critique may involve further explanation and demonstration by the instructor of the correct procedure or technique.

Application of the Skill

The final factor applicable to the learning of a skill is recognition by a trainee of when and where to apply the skill. Trainees should not only learn a skill so that it becomes easy, almost instinctive to perform; they must also learn to recognise the situations when the performance of the skill is appropriate or otherwise.

The Transfer of Learning

Learning a skill may be affected by previous mental or physical activity in another skill. This is called transfer of learning, but like motivation, it can be positive or negative.

If proficiency in a previously learned skill helps the learning of a new skill, **positive habit transfer** occurs. For example, a trainee with previous sailing experience may progress more rapidly as a trainee pilot because of existing knowledge of aerodynamic principles and navigation.

However, proficiency in a previously learned skill may inhibit the learning of a new skill; in this case, **negative habit transfer** has occurred. For example, a bobcat driver is used to pushing and pulling levers and pedals may have difficulty in relearning muscle memory actions in controlling a helicopter.

An instructor can often predict the probability and possible effect of learning transfer if a trainee's previous experience is known. This knowledge can be used to aid the learning process by making full use of positive habit transfer, and by planning instruction to minimise negative habit transfer.

Habit Formation

Effective learning is aided if trainees are encouraged to form good habit patterns from the beginning of the learning process.

For example:

Trainees should be encouraged to habitually revise essential knowledge between lessons by reading appropriate references, to organise their time so that every element of a training program is adequately covered, and to ensure that they receive an adequate briefing before each practice session.

Psychology of Learning

The following extracts summarise:

- Maslow's Hierarchy of Needs theory
- Douglas McGregor's X and Y theory
- Fredick Herzberg two factor theory

These are all required knowledge for the PIRC.

The relationship between an instructor and a trainee is a critical factor in the learning process. Trainees expect an instructor not only to teach but also to guide them towards their learning goals. This guidance requires that the instructor have some understanding of human behaviour and some knowledge of how to control that behaviour. The instructor's challenge is to recognise which controls are best applied in particular circumstances, which should be based on more than just trial and error.

> **Recommended Reading:**
> Aviation Instructor's Handbook: *Chapter 2 - Human Behaviour*[10]

Maslow's Hierarchy of Needs

All humans have similar needs. In the 1950s Abraham Maslow organised these basic human needs into levels of importance referred to as Maslow's hierarchy of human needs.

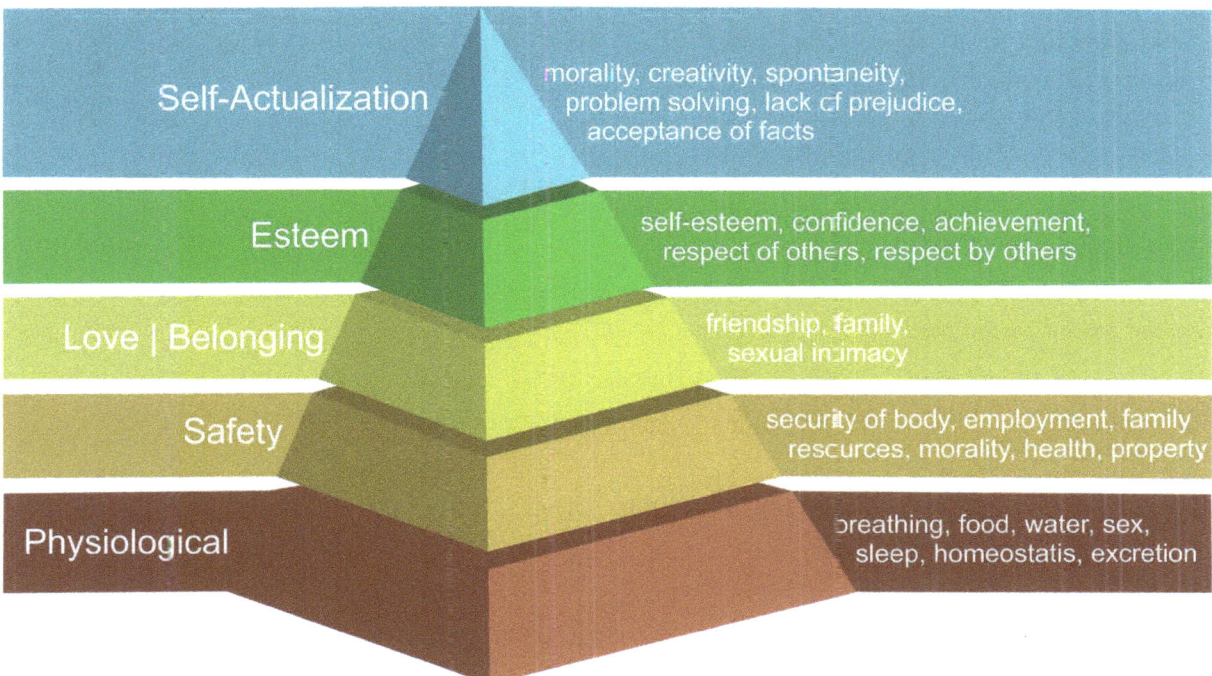

Understanding the hierarchy of needs will help the instructor manage the trainee.

---

[10] https://www.faa.gov/regulations_policies/handbooks_manuals/aviation/aviation_instructors_handbook/media/04_aih_chapter_2.pdf

Physiological

Before the learning process can start the trainee must have satisfied their physical needs of food, rest and shelter. Instructors need to monitor the trainee to ensure that they are not tired or hungry which would degrade their ability to perform and learn.

Safety

The trainee needs to feel safe, that is they are protected from danger, threats and deprivation to be able to learn. Poor maintenance, a dangerous instructor, a lack of systems and processes can degrade the trainee's perception of safety and will in turn degrade their ability to learn.

Love and belonging (Social)

Once the physical and safety needs are met a trainee will seek to meet their social needs and will need to feel part of the group.

Belonging to the aviation fraternity and how they fit in can be influenced by the instructor.

Esteem

A trainee will need to satisfy their ego. This can be driven in two ways:

- Ego as it relates to the trainee's self-esteem, their self-confidence, independence, achievement, competence, and knowledge, and
- Ego as it relates to the trainee's reputation, status, recognition and respect of their peers.

When an instructor knows what is driving a trainee, they can use the esteem part of the hierarchy of needs to assist in the learning process

Self-Actualisation

At the top of the hierarchy of needs is self-actualisation also referred to as self-fulfilment. This is when the trainee realises their potential for continued development.

Instructors should strive to help trainees satisfy their basic human needs in a manner that will create a healthy learning environment. Fulfilling the above needs will mean the instructor and the trainee experience fewer frustrations.

Douglas McGregor's X and Y Theory

Background

Theory X and Theory Y are theories of human motivation, created by psychologist Douglas McGregor in the 1960s. They describe two contrasting models for worker motivation. He pioneered the argument that workers are not merely cogs in the company machinery.

The theories look at how a manager's perceptions of what motivates his or her team members affect the way he or she behaves. By understanding how your assumptions about employees' motivation can influence your management style, you can adapt your approach appropriately, and so manage people more effectively.

Understanding the Theories

Each person's management style is strongly influenced their beliefs and assumptions about what motivates a team: If you believe that someone dislikes work, you will tend towards an authoritarian style of management; On the other hand, if you believe that someone takes pride in doing a good job, you will tend to adopt a more participative style.

Understanding your assumptions about trainee motivation can help you learn to manage and instruct more effectively.

A Simple Overview Diagram

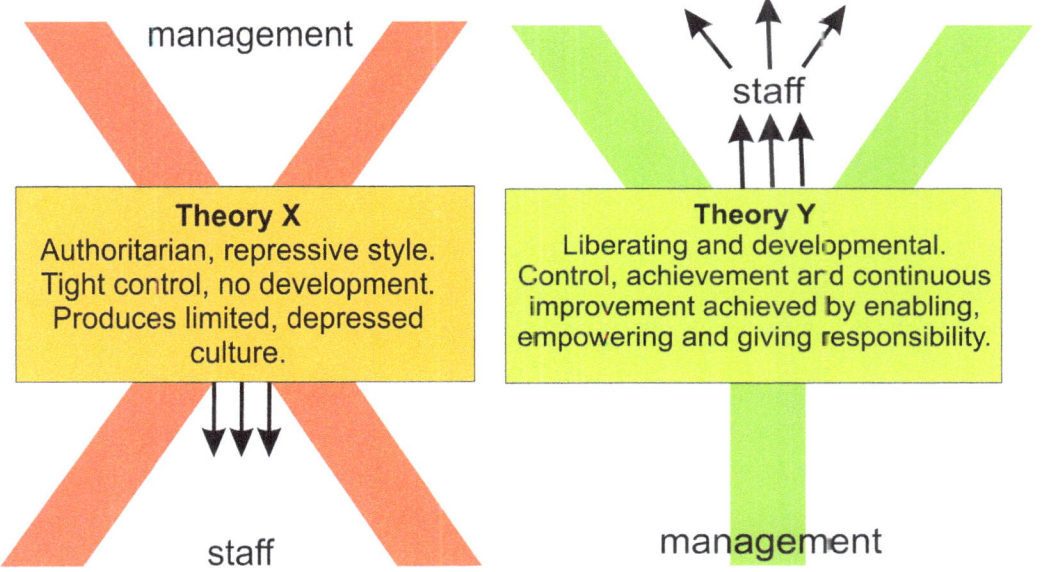

Adapted from McGregor, D, 2002, Theory X and Theory Y, Workforce, Vol.81, Issue 1

A Quick comparison

Theory x ('authoritarian management' style)	Theory y ('participative management' style)
<ul><li>The average person dislikes work and will avoid it if he/she can.</li><li>Therefore, most people must be forced with the threat of punishment to work towards organisational objectives.</li><li>The average person prefers to be directed; to avoid responsibility; is relatively unambitious and wants security above all else.</li></ul>	<ul><li>People are happy to work, are self-motivated and creative, and enjoy working with greater responsibility.</li><li>People will apply self-control and self-direction in the pursuit of organisational objectives, without external control or the threat of punishment.</li><li>Commitment to objectives is a function of rewards associated with their achievement.</li><li>People usually accept and often seek responsibility.</li><li>The capacity to use a high degree of imagination, ingenuity, and creativity in solving organisational problems is widely, not narrowly, distributed in the population.</li><li>In industry the intellectual potential of the average person is only partly utilised.</li></ul>

Comparing Theory X and Theory Y

Motivation

Theory X assumes that people dislike working; they want to avoid it and do not want to take responsibility. Theory Y assumes that people are self-motivated and thrive on responsibility.

Management Style and Control

In a Theory X organisation, management is authoritarian, and centralised control is retained, whilst in Theory Y, the management style is participative: Management involves employees in decision making but retains the power to implement decisions.

Work Organisation

Theory X employees tend to have specialised and often repetitive work. In Theory Y, the work tends to be organised around wider areas of skill or knowledge; Employees are also encouraged to develop expertise and make suggestions and improvements.

Rewards and Appraisals

Theory X organisations work on a 'carrot and stick' basis, and performance appraisal is part of the overall mechanisms of control and remuneration. In Theory Y organisations, appraisal is also regular and important but is usually a separate mechanism from organisational controls. Theory Y organisations also give employees frequent opportunities for promotion.

Application

Although Theory X management style is widely accepted as inferior to others, it has its place in large scale production operations and unskilled production-line work. Many of the principles of Theory Y are widely adopted by types of organisations that value and encourage participation. Theory Y-style management is suited to knowledge work and professional services. Professional service organisations naturally evolve Theory Y-type practices by the nature of their work; Even highly structured knowledge work, such as call centre operations, can benefit from Theory Y principles to encourage knowledge sharing and continuous improvement.

Exercise

Take time to think through your own work experiences.

- Which approach do you prefer?
- Do you work most effectively when your boss controls every part of everything you do? Or would this drive you mad, so that you'd just do what he or she wanted (and nothing more), look for another job, and then leave? Or would you prefer a boss who helps you to do your best, increasingly trusts your judgment, allows you to use your creativity, and step-by-step gives you more control over your job?
- Would you work more effectively for a Theory X or Theory Y manager?

Summary

Mix and Match

Different people, even members of your team may have different attitudes. Many may thrive on Theory Y management, while others may need Theory X management. Still, others may benefit from an altogether different approach.

Mix and match appropriately.

Fredick Herzberg Two Factor Theory

What do people want from their jobs?

Do they want just a higher salary? Or do they want security, good relationships with co-workers, opportunities for growth and advancement – or something else altogether?

This is an important question because it's at the root of motivation, the art of engaging with members of your team in such a way that they give their very best performance.

The psychologist Fredrick Herzberg asked the same question in the 1950s and 60s as a means of understanding employee satisfaction. He set out to determine the effect of attitude on motivation, by asking people to describe situations where they felt really good, and bad, about their jobs. What he found was that people who felt good about their jobs gave very different responses from the people who felt bad.

These results form the basis of Herzberg's Motivation-Hygiene Theory (sometimes known as Herzberg's Two Factor Theory.) Published in his famous article "One More Time: How do You Motivate Employees", the conclusions he drew were extraordinarily influential, and still form the bedrock of good motivational practice nearly half a century later.

Motivation-Hygiene Theory

Herzberg's findings revealed that certain characteristics of a job are consistently related to job satisfaction, while different factors are associated with job dissatisfaction. These are:

Factors for Satisfaction	Factors for Dissatisfaction
<ul><li>Achievement</li><li>Recognition</li><li>The work itself</li><li>Responsibility</li><li>Advancement</li><li>Growth</li></ul>	<ul><li>Company policies</li><li>Supervision</li><li>Relationship with supervisor and peers</li><li>Work conditions</li><li>Salary</li><li>Status</li><li>Security</li></ul>

Adapted from 'One More Time: How do You Motivate Employees?' by Frederick Herzberg. Harvard Business Review © 1968.

The conclusion he drew is that job satisfaction and job dissatisfaction are not opposites.

- The opposite of **Satisfaction** is **No Satisfaction**.
- The opposite of **Dissatisfaction** is **No Dissatisfaction**.

Remedying the causes of dissatisfaction will not create satisfaction. Nor will adding the factors of job satisfaction eliminate job dissatisfaction. If you have a hostile work environment, giving someone a promotion will not make him or her satisfied. If you create a healthy work environment but do not provide members of your team with any of the satisfaction factors, the work they're doing will still not be satisfying.

According to Herzberg, the factors leading to job satisfaction are "separate and distinct from those that lead to job dissatisfaction." Therefore, if you set about eliminating dissatisfying job factors you may create peace, but not necessarily enhance performance. This placates your workforce instead of motivating them to improve performance.

The characteristics associated with job dissatisfaction are called hygiene factors. When these have been adequately addressed, people will not be dissatisfied, nor will they be satisfied. If you want to motivate your team, you then have to focus on satisfaction factors like achievement, recognition, and responsibility.

Principles and Methods of Instruction *for Helicopter Pilots*

A Simple Diagram

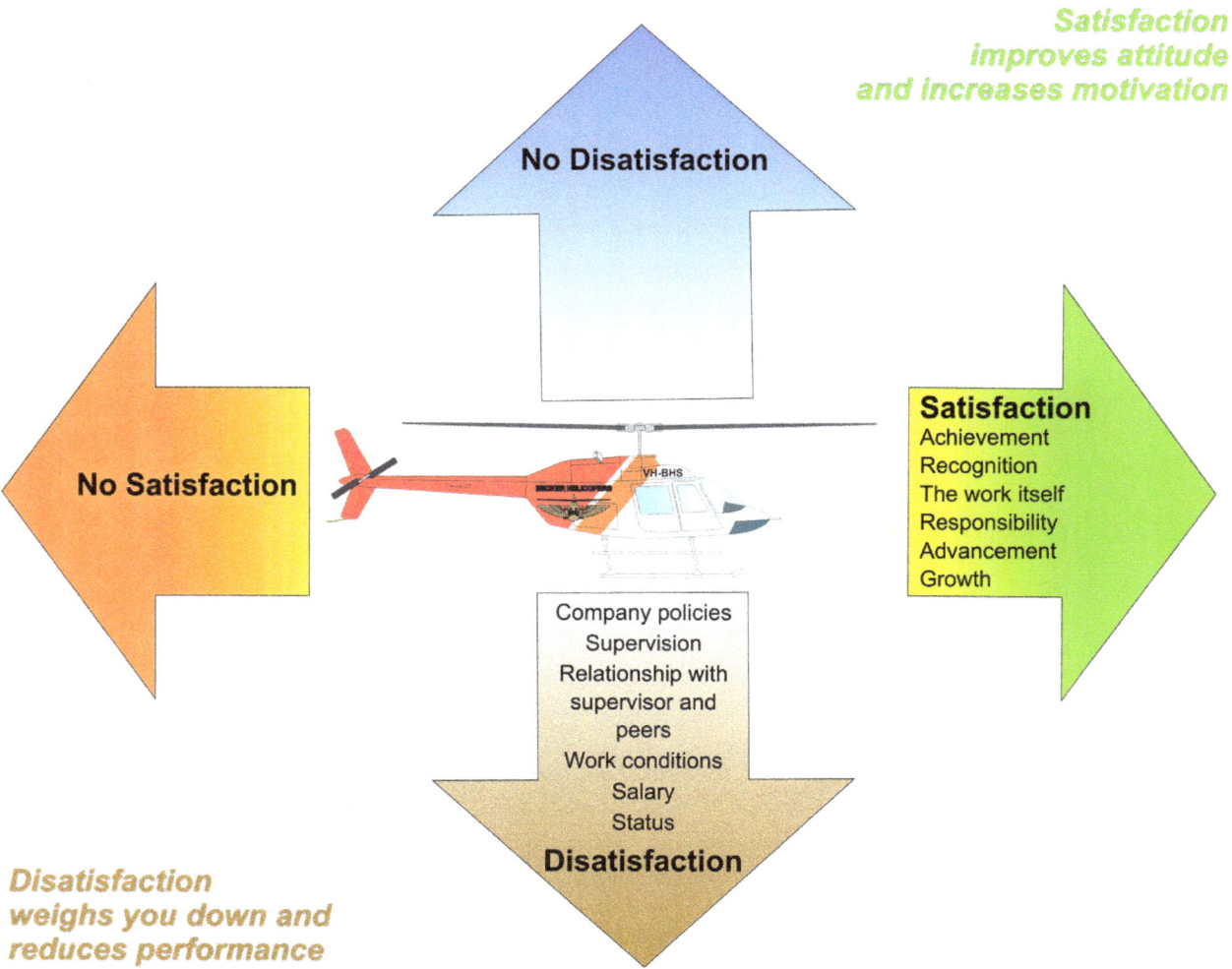

Note:

Despite its wide acceptance, Herzberg's theory has its detractors. Some say its methodology does not address the notion that when things are going well people tend to look at the things they enjoy about their job. When things are going badly, however, they tend to blame external factors.

Another common criticism is the fact that the theory assumes a strong correlation between job satisfaction and productivity. Herzberg's methodology did not address this relationship, therefore this assumption needs to be correct for his findings to have practical relevance.

To apply the theory, you need to adopt a two-stage process to motivate people. Firstly, you need to eliminate the dissatisfactions they're experiencing and, secondly, you need to help them find satisfaction.

Step One: Eliminate Job Dissatisfaction

Herzberg called the causes of dissatisfaction "hygiene factors". To get rid of them, you need to:

- Fix poor and obstructive company policies.
- Provide effective, supportive and non-intrusive supervision.
- Create and support a culture of respect and dignity for all team members.
- Ensure that wages are competitive.
- Build job status by providing meaningful work for all positions.
- Provide job security.

All of these actions help you eliminate job dissatisfaction in your organisation. And there's no point trying to motivate people until these issues are out of the way!

You can't stop there, though. Remember, just because someone is not dissatisfied, it doesn't mean he or she is satisfied either! Now you have to turn your attention to building job satisfaction.

Step Two: Create Conditions for Job Satisfaction

To create satisfaction, Herzberg says you need to address the motivating factors associated with work. He called this "job enrichment". His premise was that every job should be examined to determine how it could be made better and more satisfying to the person doing the work. Things to consider include:

- Providing opportunities for achievement.
- Recognising workers' contributions.
- Creating work that is rewarding and that matches the skills and abilities of the worker.
- Giving as much responsibility to each team member as possible.
- Providing opportunities to advance in the company through internal promotions.
- Offering training and development opportunities, so that people can pursue the positions they want within the company.

Tip 1:

Here we're approaching the subject of motivation in a very general way. In reality, you'll need "different strokes for different folks" – in other words, different people will perceive different issues, and will be motivated by different things. Make sure you talk with your people regularly on a one-to-one basis to find out what matters to them.

Tip 2:

This theory is largely responsible for the practice of allowing people greater responsibility for planning and controlling their work, as a means of increasing motivation and satisfaction.

Key Points

The relationship between motivation and job satisfaction is not overly complex. The problem is that many employers look at the hygiene factors as ways to motivate when in fact, beyond the very short term, they do very little to motivate.

Perhaps managers like to use this approach because they think people are more financially motivated than, perhaps, they are, or perhaps it just takes less management effort to raise wages than it does to re-evaluate company policy and redesign jobs for maximum satisfaction.

When you're seeking to motivate people, firstly get rid of the things that are annoying them about the company and the workplace. Make sure they're treated fairly, and with respect.

Once you've done this, look for ways in which you can help people grow within their jobs, give them opportunities for achievement, and praise that achievement wherever you find it.

Apply This to Your Life

If you lead a team, take a little time with each of the members of your team to check that they're happy, that they think they're being fairly and respectfully treated, and that they're not being affected by unnecessary bureaucracy.

You may be horrified by what you find once you start probing (bureaucracy, in particular, has a way of spreading), but you may be able to improve things quickly if you put your mind to it.

Then find out what they want from their jobs, do what you can to give this to them, and help them grow as individuals.

If you do this systematically, you'll be amazed by the impact this has on motivation!

Principles and Methods of Instruction *for Helicopter Pilots*

Summary

The following generalisations about motivating human behaviour give some guidance on the way an instructor may usefully exercise control of trainee behaviour having read the paragraphs above.

- A motivated person does not dislike work, provided it is a source of pleasure and satisfaction. If work is not a source of satisfaction, it will be avoided.
- A motivated person will exercise self-direction and self-control in pursuing goals to which they are committed.
- Commitment to goals is directly related to the perceived rewards associated with their achievement; the most significant reward is probably the satisfaction of ego.
- A motivated person will not only accept but will usually seek responsibility. The shirking of responsibility is not a natural human condition; it is usually the consequence of a previous unpleasant experience.
- Most human beings, irrespective of education, have a high level of intellectual ability.

Defence Mechanisms

People demonstrate defence mechanisms when they react to the realities of unpleasant situations. People use these defences to soften feelings of failure and guilt or to protect feelings of personal worth and adequacy.

Because they involve some self-deception and distortion of reality, defence mechanisms can be a hindrance to learning. These mechanisms often act at a relatively subconscious level, and therefore they may not be subject to normal conscious control. Common defence mechanisms are:

- Rationalisation
- Flight
- Aggression
- Resignation

Rationalisation

Trainees who are experiencing problems in the learning process may rationalise their problems by substituting some believable excuse for the real reason, which may be that they lack the skill or knowledge to perform adequately at that time. Few people like to admit that they lack ability, or have made a mistake. If the rationalisation is subconscious, the person sincerely believes that the excuse is real and justifiable.

Flight

Trainees may try to escape from frustrating, unpleasant or threatening situations by taking mental or physical flight. The threat is often the fear of failure, with the subsequent loss of self-esteem.

Physical flight may manifest itself as illness, which gives a person an excuse for not facing a situation they wish to avoid.

Mental flight is commonly manifested as daydreaming, which provides a simple and satisfying escape from problems.

Aggression

Anger is a normal human emotion. However, it may also be used as a defence mechanism to mask a feeling of guilt, frustration or inadequacy. In a learning situation, aggression may take the form of refusal to take part in, or an attempt to disrupt group activity.

Resignation

In the ultimate, trainees may become so frustrated or threatened by failure to progress that they lose all motivation and give up.

Stress and Anxiety

Stress and anxiety can be the most significant psychological factors affecting flight instruction and are closely related.

Anxiety, as it relates to aviation, can be defined as a state of uneasiness or tension caused by apprehension of possible future misfortune, danger or worry. Anxiety can often be accompanied by physical symptoms such as shaking and intense feelings in the gut.

Stress, as it relates to aviation, can be defined as a mentally or emotionally disruptive or upsetting condition occurring in response to adverse external influences and capable of affecting physical health, usually characterised by increased heart rate, a rise in blood pressure, muscular tension, irritability, and depression.

It is normal for Trainees to experience some form of anxiety or stress. What they have to learn is how to recognise and manage it.

Normal reactions to stress

When a Trainee is put under pressure and recognises a Threat or an Error, whether it be real or imagined, the brain will alert the body which will have a physiological response such as an increase in the heart rate, a rush of adrenalin, faster breathing all in preparation for the body to respond to the threat or error.

Normal Trainees will manage this response and will respond within the limits of their experience and training.

Abnormal reaction to stress

Some trainees will not manage their reaction to stress and instead may make illogical or inappropriate responses.

Extreme over-cooperation, painstaking self-control, inappropriate laughing or singing, rapid changes in emotions, marked changes in mood, anger at the instructor are all signs of an abnormal reaction to stress.

Seriously abnormal reaction to stress

If an instructor believes that a trainee has a serious psychological problem, particularly when put under stress, then the following steps are to be conducted:

- Ask another senior instructor to review the student.
- Refer that student to the head of training operations.
- Do not fly with the trainee until the psychological issue has been resolved to your satisfaction.

The Instructor's Role in Human Relations

Instructors can do a great deal to control trainee behaviour by helping them to satisfy their goals, develop their potential abilities and overcome the subconscious use of defence mechanisms. The instructor should follow several rules to achieve these objectives:

- Keep trainees motivated
- Keep trainees informed
- Treat trainees as individuals
- Give credit which it is due
- Criticise constructively
- Be consistent; and
- Admit errors.

Keep Trainees Motivated.

Because motivation is such a major factor in learning, loss of motivation is a major problem. An instructor should identify a trainee's real motivation(s) for gaining skill and knowledge, and then continue to stimulate that motivation as training progresses. This is particularly important when the inevitable "plateaus" occur.

Principles and Methods of Instruction *for Helicopter Pilots*

Keep trainees Informed

Trainees feel insecure if they are uncertain of their progress, or if they are confronted by the unexpected. Trainees must always be given adequate notice of assignments or tests, and mentally prepared for them.

Treat Trainees as Individuals

In a group-learning situation, treat each trainee as an individual. Do not ascribe a "group personality" to all the trainees.

Give Credit When It Is Due

Reward hard work and success with praise for the performance. Without this explicit recognition of achievement, trainees become frustrated. However, praise given too freely soon becomes valueless, and it should therefore be used wisely to stimulate further achievement.

Criticise Constructively

Simple identification of mistakes is not good instruction. Mistakes should be carefully analysed to determine the reasons behind them, and a trainee should then be guided to overcome the problem. Criticism should only be used to improve performance, never to belittle.

Be Consistent

Apart from satisfying their ego, trainees will normally try to please an instructor. However, they need to know what is expected of them. In specifying required performance, an instructor must be consistent, to avoid trainee confusion and frustration.

Admit Errors

No one, not even trainees, expects instructors to be perfect. Instructors who are prepared to acknowledge their fallibility and admit mistakes will gain the respect of their trainees and enhance their position in the trainee/instructor relationship. On the other hand, instructors who deny errors will quickly destroy their credibility and lose the respect of their trainees. Once respect and credibility are lost, the prospect of successful learning in that relationship is minimal.

Barriers To Effective Communication

The nature of language and visual images, and how they used often leads to misunderstandings and ineffective communication. These misunderstandings normally stem from the existence of three barriers to effective communication:

Lack of a common core of experience

Words (and sometimes visual images) rarely carry precisely the same meaning in the mind of the communicator (source) and the mind of the receiver. Words and visual images (symbols) are merely stimuli to arouse a response in the mind of the receiver. The nature of this response is determined by the receiver's previous experience with the symbols and their meanings.

The source (usually the instructor) and the receiver (usually the trainee) must share some common core of experience so that the symbols used will have the same meanings to both. This core of experience is built as training progresses, but a lack of some common core of experience, in the beginning, can create a barrier to effective communication in the early stages of training.

What the Trainee hears
OK Mohammed blah blah blah blah, blah blah blah blah blah blah blah ERSA blah blah blah blah blah blah blah blah blah blah blah VHF radio blah blah .blah blah blah blah blah blah ground blah blah blah blblah blah ah ATIS blah blah blah blah run-up blah blah blah blah blah, understand?

What the instructor says
OK Mohammed what I want you to do is find the radio frequency in the ERSA and then dial up the frequency on the primary VHF radio. Once you have done that I want you to transmit to the ground and tell them exactly what you want to do, but you have to get the ATIS first and run through all the run-up procedures, do you understand?

Confusion between the symbols used and what is being symbolised.

In choosing symbols (words or visual images) to use in the communication process, the instructor must ensure that they accurately represent what is being symbolised. If the subject is difficult to symbolise realistically, the instructor must ensure that the trainee understands the difference between the symbols used and reality.

Overuse of abstractions.

Abstract words and visual images are often used to describe or explain a general concept or philosophy without finer detail. Unfortunately, abstractions normally require considerable thought and imagination on the part of the trainee to fully understand their meaning. The overuse of abstracts can lead to misunderstanding and slow the communication process as the trainee tries to imagine what the words or images really mean.

If abstractions must be used, they should be accompanied by examples or illustrations to make their meaning clear. However, words or images which have clear, concrete, precise meaning should be used whenever possible.

The Teaching Process

> **Recommended Reading:**
>
> Aviation Instructor's Handbook: *Chapter 4 – Effective Communication*[11] and *Chapter 5 The Teaching Process*[12]

For effective learning to occur there must be an effective teaching process. Teaching may be done in a number of ways. A person may be "self-taught" by reading, watching and applying. The watching may involve the real word or audio-visual media such as DVDs or YouTube. The application may simply be a matter of trial and error experimentation, or the practice of skills, knowledge and behaviours learned to gain proficiency.

However, the most effective method of teaching is usually by listening to and watching an "expert." That is a person who possesses the desired skills, knowledge and behaviours, and who also has the teaching ability to transfer these skills, knowledge and behaviours to the trainees who can practice under "expert" supervision. This is the method used for teaching the skills, knowledge and behaviours associated with flying.

Effective Communication

For effective teaching, there must be effective communication between the instructor (expert) and the trainee. All processes of communication involve three basic elements.

A Source or Transmitter

The instructor (expert) is normally the **source** in the communication process. Effectiveness in this role depends on:

- An ability to select and use language, which has meaning to the trainee.
- The instructor's attitude to the subject, which must create the impression that what is being communicated is of value to the trainee; and
- An ability to convey an impression of expertise in the subject without resorting to technical jargon, which may have little meaning to the trainee.

The Symbols or Language

Communication is achieved by the use of symbols or language, normally using either written, aural or visual media. Effective communication requires not only the selection and use of the most appropriate symbols and language, but also the selection of the most effective media to transmit the symbols. Preferably a combination of media, usually written, aural and visual, should be used.

In learning physical skills such as flying, touch is also an important medium. As with electronic communication, the source (instructor) must try to ensure that there is no other "noise" (distractions) on the communication channels used, which might "garble" the symbols.

The Receiver

The trainee is usually the receiver in the communication process, although effective communication is a two-way process. Success in the communication process requires that the source (trainee) understands the ability of the receiver to recognise, interpret and use the symbols transmitted.

---

[11] https://www.faa.gov/regulations_policies/handbooks_manuals/aviation/aviation_instructors_handbook/media/06_aih_chapter_4.pdf

[12] https://www.faa.gov/regulations_policies/handbooks_manuals/aviation/aviation_instructors_handbook/media/07_aih_chapter_5.pdf

Phases in the Teaching Process

Each session in the teaching process should be broken into four phases:

- Preparation
- Presentation
- Application, and
- Review, Evaluate and Critique.

Preparation

An instructor must first determine what is to be covered in each lesson, the objectives to be achieved and the teaching method to be used. Research is then normally conducted to ensure that the instructor is thoroughly familiar with the subject of the lesson and that only material appropriate to the lesson is included. As part of the preparation, the instructor must check that any required material and resources needed for the lesson are available. All of this preparation should culminate in a written lesson plan, which the instructor can use as a guide in the next phase.

Presentation

In this phase, the instructor presents the skills, knowledge and behaviours, which he wishes the trainees to learn to achieve the lesson objectives. The choice of presentation method will depend upon the nature of the subject. In aviation, the instructor will generally use a whiteboard, presentation, video, practical training aid or some other means to deliver the material either to a large group right down to a one on one session.

Application

In this phase, the trainee applies (practices) what has been learned, usually under instructor supervision. This is a vital phase in the teaching process; where trainee activity is a prerequisite to effective learning, without it, an instructor has no idea that learning has taken place and cannot identify and correct mistakes.

Application may be integrated into the presentation phase, or be conducted separately. In purely theoretical lessons, application usually takes the form of questions or problems and solutions to check that learning objectives are being achieved.

Review, Evaluation and Critique

Each lesson should conclude with a review or summary, then an evaluation to ensure that the lesson objectives have been achieved and finally a critique of the trainee's performance. If the application phase is integrated with the presentation, the evaluation and critique are normally also integrated into this phase. The timing of the evaluation and critique will depend on the teaching method used.

Teaching Methods

Teaching methods are the means by which instructors transfer their skills, knowledge and attitudes to their trainees. An instructor's effectiveness is largely determined by their ability to organise material and to select the teaching method, which is most appropriate to the subject and their trainees' aptitudes.

The teaching methods covered in this course are:

- The lesson method (normally referred to as the Long Brief or Mass Brief),
- The discussion method (applicable to pre- and post-flight briefings)
- The Thumbnail brief (used for short bursts of information) and
- The demonstration, direct and monitor (performance) method used for the teaching of skills in the aircraft.

Recommended Reading:

Aviation Instructor's Handbook: *Chapter 7 – Planning Instructional Activity*[13]

The Lesson

Each lesson usually has limited objectives and is part of a logical progression through a syllabus of training. Each lesson is therefore naturally linked to the one before and the one after and is identified in the applicable syllabus of training.

Each lesson should last no longer than forty-five (45) minutes to one (1) hour, as this is generally regarded as the limit of mental concentration, even for the highly motivated trainee. To help ensure that the subject is fully and logically covered in the time allocated, a lesson plan is used to guide the instructor during the lesson and organises the lesson into a logical process of Introduction, Development and Conclusion.

Lesson Introduction

The lesson introduction is designed to prepare the trainee for the development of the lesson and set the scene for effective learning. As a guide to planning the introduction, the mnemonic **INTROSH** can be used.

Item	Description
Interest	The trainee's interest in the subject should be stimulated. This can be done by the instructor relating an experience or example to generate the interest.
Need	In stimulating interest, the instructor should also ensure that the trainee knows why he/she needs the skill or knowledge, which is the subject of the lesson. This can sometimes be done effectively by again relating a short story or example, which clearly demonstrates the need.
Title	Each lesson should have a clear title describing the subject. This title is usually taken from the course syllabus and should be displayed throughout the lesson.
Review/Link	The introduction should establish a link with the previous lesson, and review any key points, which are important to the development and understanding of the current lesson. This review can be conducted effectively by asking a small number of questions to start trainee involvement and to determine that essential knowledge or mental skill still exists.

---

[13] https://www.faa.gov/regulations_policies/handbooks_manuals/aviation/aviation_instructors_handbook/media/09_aih_chapter_7.pdf

Item	Description
Objectives	Most importantly, the introduction must specify the objectives of the lesson, that is, how the instructor expects the trainee(s) to demonstrate that they have gained the knowledge and skills required for the lesson to be regarded as successful.
Scope	The instructor should briefly describe what is to be covered and how the lesson is to be developed. This is usually best done after the objectives have been identified.
Handouts	Before beginning the development of the lesson, the instructor should advise the trainee(s) whether they will need to take any notes, or whether (preferably) a handout will be given. A handout usually allows the trainee to follow the lesson as it progresses and make relevant notes of essential knowledge and references for further study.

The introduction to a lesson should last no longer than about 10 minutes, and be separate from the development so that trainees know when the lesson proper has begun.

Lesson Development

The instructor should plan to develop the lesson in a logical manner, which will enable the trainee's insight to occur quickly and easily. Logical relationships between the parts of a lesson will normally use one of the following methods:

Chronological Development

For some subject matter, the most appropriate method of development is chronological, that is, in the order in which events occur. This method is most appropriate to a pre-flight briefing, where a particular sequence of events is covered.

Simple to Complex

This method is used where the learning of a relatively complex concept can best be learned by first understanding relatively simple basic principles, which are then combined into a complex whole. The learning of subjects such as Principles of Flight, Navigation, etc normally uses this method of lesson development.

Known to Unknown

When an instructor is sure of a trainee's existing knowledge, lesson development can be planned to logically extend this knowledge to new areas. This method provides an ideal opportunity for maximum trainee activity, as the trainee(s) can be guided to use existing knowledge to develop comprehension of new ideas, principles or concepts.

Theory to Application

This method first covers the theoretical basis for practical activity. This is the method most used for extended briefings in flying training. Theoretical concepts, such as aerodynamics, which are relevant to the next flying lesson, are developed first and then the practical application of this theory is developed.

Depending on the length of the lesson and the complexity of the subject, periodic summaries may be included in the development of the lesson. The most effective summaries use visual techniques. The summaries may also be used for a progressive evaluation of the lesson objectives.

Conclusion

Every lesson must have an effective conclusion. The conclusion should summarise the key points covered in the development, and then evaluate the achievement of the objectives by asking direct questions or by conducting a short written test. The extent of this final evaluation will depend on whether a progressive evaluation has already been conducted. Finally, trainees should be given any handouts, be told how this lesson is linked to their next activity, and be advised of any self-study or revision required in preparation for their next lesson.

Principles and Methods of Instruction *for Helicopter Pilots*

Aviation Lessons

In aviation, there is a standard format followed when delivering a lesson for a flying sortie.

The order of the information flow is:

- Trainee pre-study and pre-reading relevant information given or recommended to them by the instructor
- Instructor delivers a Long Brief of approximately 45 minutes. This may be done on the day of the flight or several days prior.
- Instructor delivers a Pre-Flight Brief of approximately 15 minutes on the same day as the flight and is a quick revision of the Long Brief as well as a discussion on the aircraft weather and training environment for the day.

Long Brief

The Long Brief will follow a standard layout even though the information within it will change based on the lesson. It will consist of a:

- Title
- Aim
- Objective/s
- Airmanship
- Preparation
- Air Exercise
- Key takeaway
- Threat Error Management (TEM)
- Revision and questions

Title

This is the name of the lesson.

Aim

This is the overall purpose or reason for the lesson. To come up with a clear aim ask the following question.

"The purpose of this lesson is to [discuss, demonstrate, introduce, revise etc] what to the trainee?"

Motivation and Revision

This is not written down on the long brief. Instead, it refers to the verbal introduction (INTROSH) given by the instructor linking the new lesson to the one before and giving the trainee a reason for paying attention. It is usually delivered after stating the Aim and before introducing the Objectives.

Objectives

These are the key competencies that the lesson is trying to achieve.

The key question to come up with here is:

"By the end of this lesson, the trainee will be able to [state, write, explain, demonstrate, draw, move etc] in the [classroom or helicopter] to the satisfaction of the instructor, what??

Usually, there are several objectives to a lesson that will be explained in the Preparation and Air Exercise sections.

Airmanship

Airmanship points are items that the instructor wants to emphasise that the trainee needs to be aware of. They can be points that are relevant to the flight or any pre or post-flight actions that may affect the flight. These are often items that are common to all lessons such as preparation, lookout, HOTO, aircraft limits, radio procedures etc, but the instructor may pay particular attention to one or more items that have proven to be issues in the past.

Preparation

This section covers relevant theory, concepts or other information that is relevant for the trainee to understand before moving onto the Air Exercise portion.

Air Exercise

This gives detail on what is to be done in flight and how it is to be done.

Key Takeaway

A Key Takeaway is a summary of something specific that the instructor wants the trainee to remember. It may not be relevant for every long brief

Threat Error Management

At the end of each lesson, the instructor and the trainee are to discuss Threats and Errors that may apply to the flight.

Threats are events, things or hazards both internal and external that can affect the flight.

An error is a mistake or omission that someone in the aircraft or external to the aircraft can make.

Once threats and errors are identified, the instructor and trainee can discuss mitigators. A mitigator is something that can be put in place or done to minimise the risk of the threat or error occurring in the first place.

Revision and Questions

This is where the instructor will ask the trainee questions to see if the objectives have been met and where the trainee can ask additional questions to clarify any content in the lesson.

Typical Layout of a Long Brief

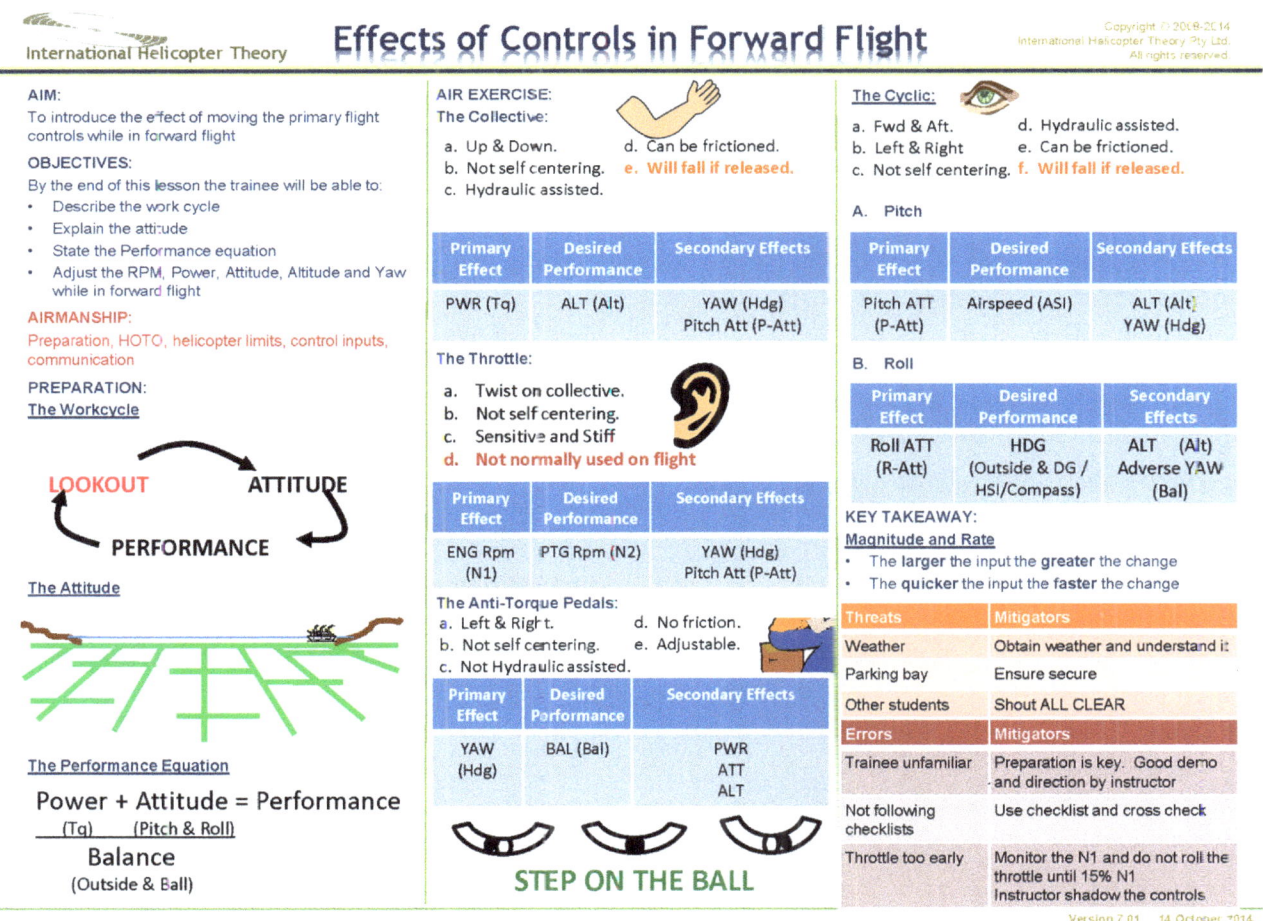

Pre-flight Brief

The Pre-flight Brief will follow a standard layout even though the information within it will change based on the lesson. The Pre-flight brief will focus on the items to be covered in that flight and will in most cases match the air exercise portion of the Long Brief.

It will consist of a:

- Title
- Aim
- Objective
- Airmanship
- Air Exercise
- Key takeaway
- Meteorology and NOTAM
- Aircraft
- Timings
- TEM (Risks)
- Emergencies (Real vs Practice)
- Revision and questions

Title

This is the name of the lesson

Aim

This is the overall purpose or reason for the lesson. To come up with a clear aim ask the following question:

"The purpose of this lesson is to demonstrate, direct and/or monitor what to the trainee?"

Motivation and Revision

This is not written down in the Pre-flight brief. Instead, it refers to the verbal introduction given by the instructor linking the new lesson to the one before and giving the trainee a reason for paying attention.

Objectives

These are the key competencies that the lesson is trying to achieve.

The key question to come up with here is:

"By the end of this lesson, the trainee will be able to [state, write, explain, demonstrate, conduct, move, etc. in the helicopter to the satisfaction of the instructor, what??

Usually, there are several objectives to a lesson.

Airmanship

Airmanship points are items that the instructor wants to emphasise that the trainee needs to be aware of. These are often items that are common to all lessons such as preparation, lookout, handover and takeover procedure, aircraft limits, radio, etc, but the instructor may pay particular attention to one or more items that have proven to be issues in the past for this particular flight.

Air Exercise

This gives detail on what is to be done in flight

Key Takeaway

A Key Takeaway is a summary of something specific that the instructor wants the trainee to remember

M.A.T.E. brief

MATE is an acronym used to guide the delivery of standard information prior to the flight

Letter	Name	Description
M	Meteorology and NOTAMs	Weather and NOTAMs are discussed and applied to the flight
A	Aircraft	Aircraft are allocated for the sortie. Location, ant maintenance issues
T	Timings	The timings are given for the sortie including - Walk time - Start time - Duration of flight - Return to base time
TEM	Threat Error Management	The instructor and trainees will list and discuss any relevant threats and errors for the flight and the mitigating strategies
E	Emergencies	Real or practice emergencies Who is in control and who will be doing what?
E	Exercise	Allocate who will be doing what - Your start and taxi - My demonstrate - Your direct and monitor - Your return to base

Revision and Questions

This is where the instructor will ask the trainee questions to see if the objectives have been met and where the trainee can ask additional questions.

Principles and Methods of Instruction *for Helicopter Pilots*

Typical Layout of a Pre-flight brief

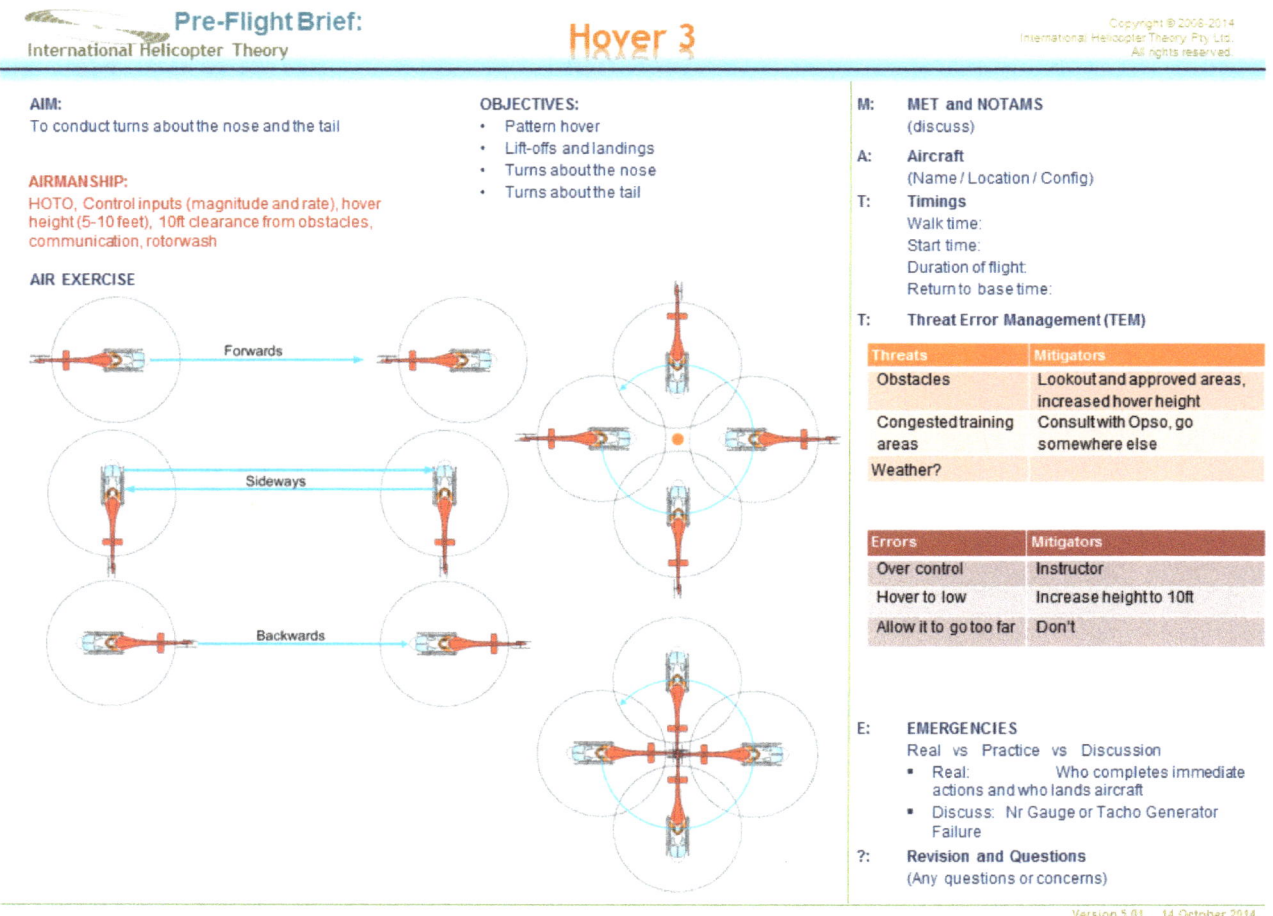

Thumbnail Brief

A Thumbnail brief is a specific quick 15-minute review on a particular topic. It allows the instructor to cover any subject matter based on the need of the trainee. It may or may not be part of a set lesson plan. It may or may not be a structured brief supplied by the school.

It is most often used when a trainee has asked a particular question and the instructor now has to answer.

Delivering a thumbnail brief is a skill the instructor needs to learn to deliver information in a manner that engages the trainee.

For example, if a trainee asks what VRS is the instructor should be able to give a quick 15-minute thumbnail brief and explain it in isolation.

Thumbnail briefs are usually not programmed within a course but are instead used as the method of delivery when there is a knowledge gap.

The instructors' personality and knowledge are used to best effect to transfer knowledge using the whiteboard.

A thumbnail brief will consist of the following:

- Title
- Aim
- Objective
- Content
- Revision and questions

Use of Lesson Plans

The forming of a lesson plan depends on several factors, the most important being the ability and experience of the instructor, and the familiarity and expertise in the subject.

An instructor who is an expert in a subject and who presents the lesson frequently may not need to constantly refer to the lesson plan. Instructors who are experienced teachers may only need a lesson plan in bare note form, a list of the elements to be covered and/or simple diagrams to prompt them. Inexperienced instructors, or those who have difficulty in finding the right words to communicate, generally need a lesson plan in near-full text form to guide them through the structure of the lesson they are about to deliver.

Companies that have large numbers of instructors and have the need to standardise the lessons will rely on Lesson Plans to ensure consistency of delivery.

The Lesson Plan used at Becker Helicopters has the following sections:

- Aim
- Duration
- Resources required
- Trainee Preparation
- Pre-requisites
- Training areas and limitations
- Aircrew configuration
- Standards
- Objectives
- Briefing and Planning
- Sortie Guide
- Emergencies
- Revision

During flight training, these lesson plans may be impractical because of their size and detail. It can be useful to abbreviate the lesson plan into a kneeboard guide which is used by the instructor as a prompt for each particular lesson.

Principles and Methods of Instruction *for Helicopter Pilots*

An example of a lesson plan is shown in *Appendix B: Example Lesson Plan - Elementary Handling 1*.

Below is an example of the same lesson plan as shown in Appendix B put into a kneeboard format as used by Becker Helicopters.

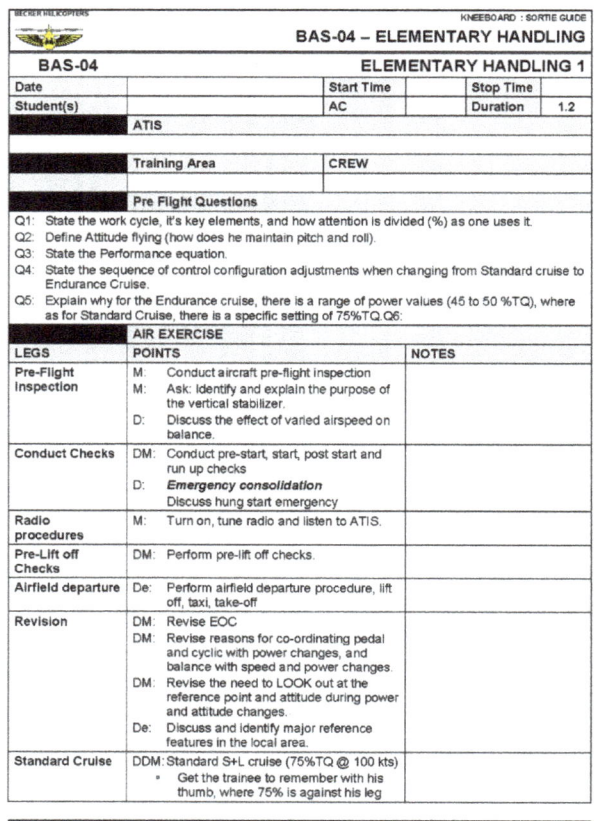
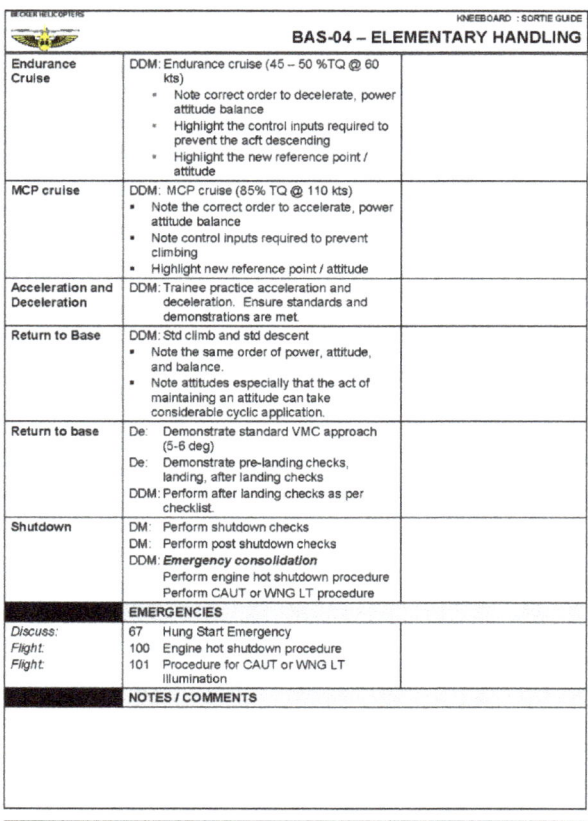

No matter what form the lesson plan takes, it should guide the instructor through a logical development of the lesson, indicate what training aids to use (and when) and prompt the instructor to make full use of trainee participation.

Adequate preparation or review of a lesson plan ensures that an instructor has effectively given him or herself the lesson before giving it to the trainee(s), promoting self-confidence and helping to dispel the fear of forgetting. An instructor who prepares and uses a lesson plan properly should never be lost for words or get off the track and will cover the subject fully in the allocated time.

Use of a lesson plan should never be hidden from trainees, or apologies offered for its use. An instructor who uses a lesson plan properly demonstrates a commendable concern that a trainee's time should not be wasted and that he or she is committed to effective teaching.

However, if a lesson plan is prepared in a full-text form, the instructor should avoid reading it verbatim. A properly prepared instructor who knows and understands the subject **must** be capable of moving away from the lesson plan text to explain or demonstrate in his or her own words to ensure trainee comprehension. If an instructor cannot do this, he or she might just as well give the trainee the lesson plan to read, and then ask questions to resolve any lack of understanding. This technique, although feasible, will diminish an instructor's credibility as a teacher and possibly jeopardise the trainee/instructor relationship.

Happily, there are very few instructors who do not become competent, relaxed and very effective in the art of teaching as they gain experience.

Question Techniques

A lesson plan should prompt an instructor to achieve maximum trainee participation, which is vital to the learning process. During a lesson or briefing, this participation usually takes the form of questions posed by the instructor. These questions serve three main purposes:

- They enable the instructor to evaluate trainee comprehension;
- They guide the trainee to deduce new facts or conclusions from existing knowledge, promoting self-esteem; and
- They maintain trainee interest and mental alertness.

Questions may be either of the *"fact"* or *"thought"* variety.

A fact question simply requires the recall of a simple fact.

For example:

"What is the Vne for the Bell206 at Sea Level on a standard day?"

Thought questions, which are much more effective in the learning process, require the trainee to analyse the question, think logically and correlate knowledge to deduce the correct answer. This process of reasoning should be encouraged as often as possible so that it becomes a habit and will be used instinctively when the trainee is confronted with an unusual situation in the absence of the instructor such as when flying solo.

For example:

"If flying in a Bell206 from Sea Level to 5000 feet where the OAT is ISA +10, what would you expect to happen to the Vne?"

The following 206B Airspeed Limitations placard is installed in helicopter serial number 3567 and subsequent.

206B AIRSPEED LIMITATIONS–KNOTS–IAS						
3000 LB GW AND BELOW						
H_p 1000 FT	OAT-°C					
	46	40	20	0	-20	-40
0	128	130	130	130	130	130
2	121	122	130	130	130	130
4	112	114	122	129	130	130
6	103	106	113	122	130	130
8	96	97	105	113	122	130
10	87	89	96	104	113	122
12	79	81	88	96	104	113
14		73	80	87	96	104
16				78	87	96
18					78	87
20						78

ABOVE 3000 LB GW						
H_p 1000 FT	OAT-°C					
	46	40	20	0	-20	-40
0	118	122	122	122	122	122
2	102	106	122	122	122	122
4	85	89	104	121	122	122
6	69	73	88	103	121	122
8	52	56	70	86	103	122
10			53	69	86	104
12				52	69	87
14					51	69
16						51

The instructor should avoid posing questions, which can be answered with a simple *"yes"* or *"no"* as this allows the lazy trainee to avoid answering and it is also a bad technique for non-native English speakers from different cultures who may just answer the question at face value and simply reply with a *"yes"* or *"no"*.

For example:

Consider an instructor who posed the question:

"Can anyone tell me how you can recognise over pitching in a helicopter?"

This could be answered with a yes or no.

Now consider an instructor who askes the same question differently

"What is an indication of the helicopter experiencing an over pitching situation?"

This cannot be answered with a yes or no but will require some thought and an answer.

Effective Questions

Effective questions should

- Have only one correct answer
- Be relevant to the subject
- Be unambiguous (no double negatives or double meanings)
- Present a mental challenge but be within the capability of the trainee to answer, and
- Centre on one idea. That is it should not cross over to cover two themes.

Pose – Pause – Pounce technique

When teaching a group of trainees, an instructor should ask questions so that all trainees must think about it. The technique used is to **POSE, PAUSE** and then **POUNCE**.

This is where the instructor will **"POSE"** or ask a question. Once asked the instructor should **PAUSE** for a moment so that the trainees have time to think about it then when ready the instructor can **"POUNCE"** or direct the question to a particular trainee.

Questions should be asked in a way that the trainee has to answer. This is a skill the instructor will have to learn.

Posing questions is not the sole prerogative of the instructor. Trainees should be encouraged to ask their own questions as part of the learning process. In answering trainee's questions, the instructor should:

- Ensure that the question is clearly understood and if necessary ask the trainee for clarification;
- Display interest in the question and frame an answer which is direct, accurate and comprehensible;
- Be sure that the question has been answered to the trainee's satisfaction;
- Avoid being diverted from the lesson subject or introducing new or complex material which is the subject of a later lesson element in which event explain to the trainee that the answer will be covered later; and
- Never give an answer which you have doubts about, if you don't know say so. Tell the trainee you will research the question and provide an answer as soon as possible, then make sure you do.

Questioning Techniques

Overhead questions

Overhead questions (also referred to as open questions) are used to activate the group's thoughts. Usually, it is a big open-ended statement.

For example:

> *"So where did we all come from?"*

This will allow the group, or at least those motivated enough within the group to start a conversation and discussion.

Rhetorical questions

Rhetorical questions do not require an answer, however, the instructor may elect to answer the question and guide the subject in a certain direction.

For example:

> *"Well if we all came from space is that where God has come from?"*
> *"Do you think he planted the idea with us or we made it up?"*

Lead-off questions

Lead-off questions are often used by the instructor to take the subject in a particular direction. This is often used to keep a discussion on topic.

For example:

> *"If we consider how large the universe is, is it fair to assume there may be life on other planets?"*

Follow-up questions

Follow-up questions are used to be clear and define a subject. They usually encompass a single idea to stimulate thoughts that relate to the matter at hand.

For example:

> *"So if we all believe there is life on another planet, how do we go about finding that planet?"*

Direct/common questions

These are questions that the instructor directs to a particular trainee to elicit a quick response.

For example:

> *"James, has an alien ever landed on earth that we know of?"*

Reverse questions

Reverse questions are where you throw the question straight back to the person who asked it. This allows that person to answer their own question by motivating their thoughts in a different direction.

For example:

> *"Has an alien ever landed on earth that we know of?"*
> *"George, that is a good question; do you think aliens have ever visited earth?"*

Relay questions

Relay questions are ongoing by breaking the core question into smaller pieces to get an interaction by trainees and for the instructor to get feedback if the trainee understands the information given.

For example:

> *"John, so has man ever travelled to another planet?"*
> *"Paul, knowing this, is it unreasonable to think that another intelligent life form has visited earth?"*

Principles and Methods of Instruction *for Helicopter Pilots*

"Ringo, How do you think they got here?"

Written Tests

Properly constructed written tests can provide an accurate means of evaluating the achievement of the training objectives for a particular lesson. They are more formal than oral questions and require more time to prepare and evaluate. On the other hand, they provide a permanent record of the trainees' progress and comprehension and give a trainee practise in exam technique, in preparation for the final subject examination.

If properly constructed, multi-choice written tests are the way to evaluate mental skills, knowledge and behaviours. They can be evaluated by anyone with access to the answers and do not discriminate against trainees who may have the knowledge and skill required, but who may have difficulty expressing themselves in writing. However, if preparing a multi-choice written test to evaluate trainee's progress, an instructor should:

- Include sufficient questions to give comprehensive coverage of the subject which will validly measure achievement of the training objectives;
- Compose possible answers which will discriminate between the differing levels of trainee knowledge and skills, that is, only one answer should be completely correct, another should be nearly correct and at least one other should identify any trainee who makes a typical mistake in the application of skill or knowledge.

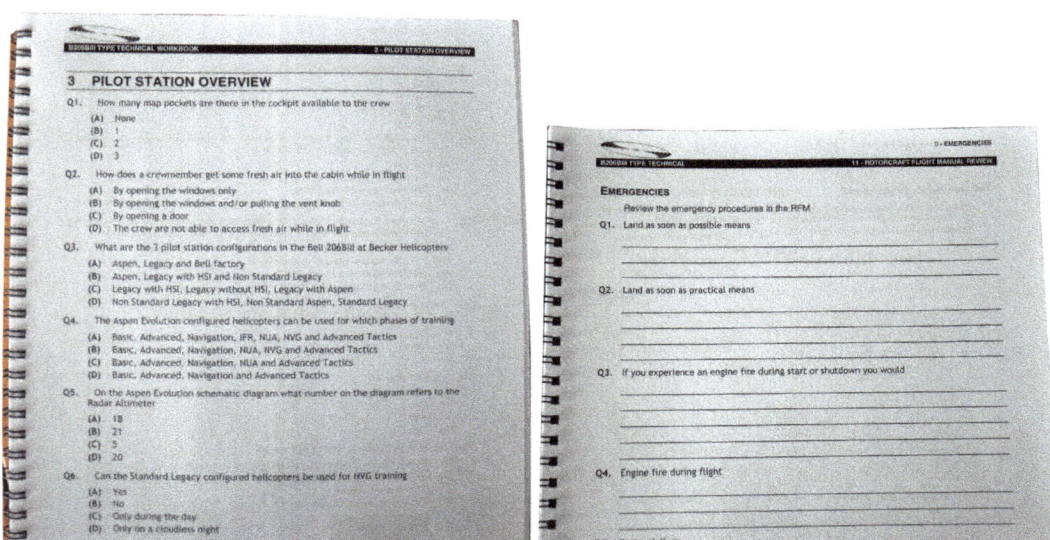

A Systems Approach to Training

Background

In the late 60's and early 70's experts in education and training around the world, particularly in the military, realised that much of the training which was being conducted was not based on a systematic, disciplined analysis of the skills, knowledge and behaviours which were required to perform the tasks for which people were being trained.

From this realisation evolved what is known as a Systems Approach to Training. This can be visualised as a closed-loop, which contains a natural progression of the elements which should be addressed in a cost-effective training process.

Task Analysis

The first element of the Systems Approach is a detailed analysis of the skills, knowledge and behaviours required to perform a particular task. The skills required are considered in terms of **mental skills** and **physical skills**.

In its most detailed form, a Task Analysis involves the survey of 'experts" (trainers, supervisors and workers) to determine what particular skills, knowledge and behaviours are required to perform a particular task. The "experts" are also required to define each task in terms of **frequency, difficulty and importance**.

The results of the survey are analysed by computer to produce a detailed list of all the skill and knowledge elements in particular tasks, and to indicate the extent and nature of training required based on frequency, difficulty and importance.

In many cases, such analysis showed that many of the skills, knowledge and behaviours which had been traditionally subject to formal and lengthy training could be learned ' on the job", while many which were identified as important and which should be the subject of "over-training" were not being taught at all!

The result of the task analysis is a syllabus of training, which should specify the actual performance required by a graduate of a training program, in terms of skill and knowledge required.

Behavioural Objectives

The next step in the Systems Approach is to specify the performance objectives to be achieved by trainees at the end of each stage of training.

The term "Behavioural Objectives" is derived from the definition of learning, that is, a change in behaviour as a result of experience.

A behavioural objective can be defined as:

"An unambiguous statement of what a trainee should be able to do as a result of training"

Objectives are specified for each level of training. Those to be achieved by the end of a training program are called **Terminal Objectives**.

Those to be achieved by the end of each training lesson are called **Enabling Objectives**.

As a flying instructor, you must be able to both interpret and construct valid objective statements.

A valid objective statement contains three elements: The **performance** to be observed, the **standard** to be achieved and the **conditions** applicable to the performance.

Performance

This part of the objective statement specifies the behaviour, which is expected as the result of training. This element of the statement must contain an "action" verb, which will identify how the acquired skill or knowledge is to be observed or evaluated.

Taking each of the categories of learning in turn:

- The statement of a physical skill element is relatively easy – we simply state what the trainee should be able to do when the training is finished.
  For example:
  "*Start an engine*" or *"maintain level flight"*.
- Stating the desired performance of a mental skill is also relatively easy
  For example:
  "*Calculate ground speed*" or *"prepare a flight plan"*.
- The statement of a knowledge performance element sometimes causes difficulties. However, these must be observable. Verbs such as "to understand" or "to know" are meaningless in objective statements, because they don't say how the trainee is to demonstrate that knowledge or understanding has been achieved. Instead, verbs such as "state", "list", "explain" or "recall" are used,
  For example:
  "*State the entry to autorotation procedure*" or "*explain how parasite drag is created*".
- Importantly, the type of performance specified must be relevant to the desired result of training.
  For example:
  Will a trainee be required "to analyse" a complex problem or "to describe" a relatively simple procedure?

Standards

By itself, a demonstration by a trainee of an observable performance is of little use as a training objective unless you and the trainee first know the standard(s) against which the performance is to be measured. By adding statements of the required standards to the examples above, the objectives become much more useful

For example:

- "Start an engine, observing all flight manual procedures and limitations"
- "Maintain level flight, +/- 100 feet and 10kts".
- "Calculate ground speed, to the nearest 5kts".
- "Prepare a flight plan, as specified in the AIP".
- "State the standard VRS recovery technique, in the correct sequence of actions and without error".
- "Explain how induced drag is created, to the satisfaction of the instructor".

Note that in the last example, the standard is specified in terms of a subjective judgement. This is a valid statement of a standard and can be used where objectively measurable standards cannot be easily or conveniently defined. However, objectively measurable standards should be used whenever possible, to ensure consistent and accurate evaluation of training.

Statements of required standards can be simplified by nominating an accepted reference to a standard such as the Part 61 Manual of Standards.

Conditions

The final element of a valid training objective is a statement of the conditions under which the trainees performance is to be observed and evaluated.

For example:

Let's complete the earlier examples by adding statements of conditions:

- *"Start a B206 engine, observing all flight manual procedures and limitations, without reference to publications".*
- *"Maintain level flight, +/- 100 feet and 10kts, in a B206 in VMC and nil turbulence".*
- *"Calculate ground speed to the nearest 5kts, given track, TAS and W/V, using a Jeppesen CR3 computer".*
- *"Prepare a flight plan as specified in the AIP, for a flight in VH-BHS from YBMC to YGYM to YBBN to YBMC direct at 5000 feet in VMC, using 75% Torque in the cruise".*
- *"State the standard VRS recovery technique from memory, in the correct sequence of actions and without error".*
- *"Without reference to notes, explain how induced drag is created, to the satisfaction of the instructor".*

To be valid, statements of standards and conditions must be realistic and relevant to the environment in which the task will be performed.

For example:

If a trainee will have access to publications when performing a task in the real world, there is little point in specifying "from memory" as a condition. Conversely, an objective requiring recall of an emergency procedure would almost certainly have "from memory" as a condition, and "without delay and error" as standards.

In practice, there is no need to pedantically state all the elements of an objective statement on every occasion. The standards and conditions may be specified for a group of objectives, as is done with our Flying Instructor Course syllabus. However, the performance element must always be specified.

Planning and Conduct of Training

Once the training objectives have been specified for each training session, the next step in the Systems Approach to Training is the planning and conduct of the actual training.

The first step is to determine which method(s) of training will best achieve the specified objectives. In the case of physical and mental skills, the demonstration/performance method is probably most appropriate. Knowledge objectives may be achieved by either formal lessons or by trainee self-study techniques; the method chosen will depend on the complexity of the subject and the intellectual background of the trainee.

In any event, a program of training must be prepared which will identify the methods to be used and the resources required. Each element of the training program must be thoroughly prepared, and instructors given adequate time to research their areas of responsibility and produce lessons plans and training aids.

Evaluation of Training

The closed-loop concept in the Systems Approach to training requires that the last step is an evaluation of the final product of the training system.

This evaluation determines that the trainee can perform the tasks which were defined in the first step, that is, that the required skills, knowledge and behaviours have been acquired. This evaluation may show that there are still some deficiencies in the system; which may require a re-analysis of the task, or modifications to the training program to include new skills, knowledge and behaviours.

The Systems Approach to Training is a dynamic, continuous process. Technology changes may require training in new skills, knowledge and behaviours, or the environment in which the task is conducted may change.

For example: New job classifications, organisational changes, etc.

All of this means that there must be a continuous process of evaluation.

Evaluation takes place at every stage of training. The instructor is observing individual trainees performance to determine if the objectives are being achieved. The training manager (CFI) is (or should be) continually evaluating instructor and trainee performance to determine if instructors need refresher or advanced training, if new training resources are needed or if the training program needs modification. In the case of civilian pilot training, the CASA and Industry Associations are continually analysing and evaluating the skills, knowledge and behaviours, which a pilot needs to safely operate modern aircraft in a changing airspace environment.

The result of this CASA/Industry evaluation may be reflected in the production of Study Guides, which modify the contents of the CASA Syllabi of Training on which School training programs are based.

Although the methods of evaluation may be either informal or formal, the ultimate goal of all evaluations at every level is to ensure that training continues to be relevant to the task for which it is designed.

Competency-based training

Now that we understand what a systems approach to training is all about we can bring in the concept of "Competency-Based Training".

In its purest form, this is where the trainee has received training and has learnt new knowledge, gained a new skill and changed their behaviour so that they are now competent to conduct the task at the required standard.

Under competency-based training, there is no requirement to have completed a minimum or a maximum number of training hours or to have been subjected to a final test that is external to the teaching process. Instead, they will train until competent and at that point be deemed to be able to now conduct the task and can be qualified.

Unfortunately in aviation, although based on a competency-based system there are still requirements to achieve minimum hours and pass tests based on traditional teaching systems.

We are in effect running two training systems in parallel. We must train the trainee until competent and if they are competent early we must continue the training whether they need it or not until they meet a minimum number of hours at which point they are eligible to undergo an external test to prove their competency.

For those that are quick learners or have other skills, knowledge or behaviours that will give positive habit transfer this can be an expensive and unnecessary burden.

For those that struggle, it will make no difference as they will train until they are competent and exceed the minimum hours anyway.

Competency-based training relies on the integrity of the Flight Schools and instructors to manage the standard to work. This is something that CASA is unwilling to allow at this time and are themselves trying to manage and monitor the standard.

Summary

1	**Task Analysis**	Identify the required skills, knowledge and behaviours required.
2	**Behavioural Objectives**	Specify the performance objectives includes the method of evaluation, standards and conditions.
3	**Planning and Conduct of Training**	Identify methods of training to best achieve the objectives, and plan the delivery of the training.
4	**Evaluation of Training**	Review the effectiveness of the training program. In a cycle of continuous improvement, modify the training program when required by returned to stage 1.

Principles and Methods of Instruction *for Helicopter Pilots*

Training Aids

Introduction

Training aids can help or hinder the instructor depending on how they are used. A training aid should assist the instructor in the teaching process by demonstrating, representing, or supporting the material being delivered. They are used intermittently throughout the lesson to give particular emphasis. Training aids are not "self-supporting". In other words, training aids are to assist instructors they do not replace them.

With advances in technology, there is continual growth and change in the capabilities and complexities of training aids. This is most obvious in the use of CBT (computer-based training) the internet, the use of video and graphics.

It is up to the instructor to find that balance in using technology to teach as opposed to the expert to teach.

Why use Training Aids

In teaching circles, it is generally agreed that the use of training aids is so effective because:

- During the communication process, the mind acts as a filter, sorting all the bits of information provided by the senses into either important or routine. Assuming this theory to be correct, the use of training aids increase the number of senses conveying it may be recognised as important.
- The brain probably tries to organise communication bits into logical arrangements. While verbal bits may require considerable effort to arrange, visual images probably simplify the process.
- After the information reaching the brain has been sorted and arranged, it must be stored for retrieval. The storage and retrieval of single visual images is probably affected more easily than the multiple bits of a verbal description. This aspect of the theory may be of particular relevance when dealing with abstract concepts or ideas.
- Research has shown that the retention of knowledge is enhanced when the instruction has involved the use of training aids providing visual support for the spoken word.
- Two further factors in the rationale for the use of training aids are that:
  - By using pre-prepared material (aids) to make concepts and ideas more quickly understood, the instructor can reduce the time spent in "teaching", and
  - By using a variety of training aids in supporting verbal teaching, the instructor will make lessons more interesting and enhance retention.

Types of Training Aids

Projection Equipment

Projection equipment has changed dramatically over the last 10 years. Overhead projectors and slide shows pretty much belong in museums. The modern trainer will use computers, DVD, the internet and projection equipment to display visual images quickly, consistently and effectively to groups of trainees or individual trainees.

Computers

Computers can be used as an effective training aid but the instructor has to ensure that they do not over-rely on this technology and forget to "teach".

Death by PowerPoint is a good way to lose a trainee and de-motivate them.

Computers can be used to deliver just about every phase of a training program including the flight portion through simulation. It is up to the instructor to find the balance between delivering material and teaching material.

Video/DVD

Taking video of lessons both on the ground and in the air is an excellent teaching aid before the lesson, during the lesson and after the lesson.

Video gives the trainee the ability to prepare, to revise and revisit a particular lesson in their own time and at their own pace.

A good quality video will have good graphics so that it is obvious what is being viewed and good sound so that the dialogue can be easily heard.

Video also has the advantage of being able to show trainees things that would not normally be able to be seen to enhance their understanding.

For example:

A slow-motion image of the rotor blade in flight as it rotates.

Video equipment must be controlled by the instructor. With the advent of smartphones, trainees are now videoing their flights which can cause them to lose concentration when being sent solo. Ensure that any video equipment is used as a training aid and not entertainment.

Non-Projection Equipment

The Whiteboard

The whiteboard is now the standard method for instructors to deliver Long Briefs when not using PowerPoint. It allows individual instructors to bring out their personality in the teaching process and to add colour and activity to the lesson. Some whiteboards are also magnetic, so magnetic cut-outs can be used to represent the helicopter or aerofoil or similar and then they can be moved around as the lesson and discussion progress.

The following are some hints and tips on how to use a whiteboard:

- Start each lesson with a clean board.
- Use colours for emphasis.
- Make lettering large enough to read – usually about 5 centimetres high.
- Organise the layout of the material; do not use the board merely as an oversize jotter.
- Strive for simplicity and neatness in layout.
- Draw then talk.
- Erase, cover or remove material that is not relevant to the current part of the lesson; do not allow the board to become cluttered and confusing.
- If using a metal whiteboard, use pre-prepared magnetic cut-outs of shapes, etc, which will be used frequently during lessons, e.g., aerofoil cross-sections, one-dimensional aircraft shapes, lift formula, etc.
- Use the following colours on the whiteboard to give a consistent approach.

Principles and Methods of Instruction *for Helicopter Pilots*

Colour	Use
■ Black	Headings, titles and wording. Axis for diagrams, aerofoils, buildings, bridges and other non-descript items.
■ Blue	Headings, aim and wording. Airflow, vectors relating to air, water and watercourses, clouds,
■ Red	Anything relating to airmanship, risk and threat error management. Drag related vectors, any safety issues, emergencies or limitations. Wording relating to emergencies or danger.
■ Green	Wording to support positive action or results. Lift related vectors, trees and foliage.
■ Orange	Weight vectors used to show a potential threat and mitigation strategies.
■ Brown	Mountain counters and terrain and ground features.
■ Purple	Torque or power vectors. Used to highlight specific points of interest not covered by other colour selections.

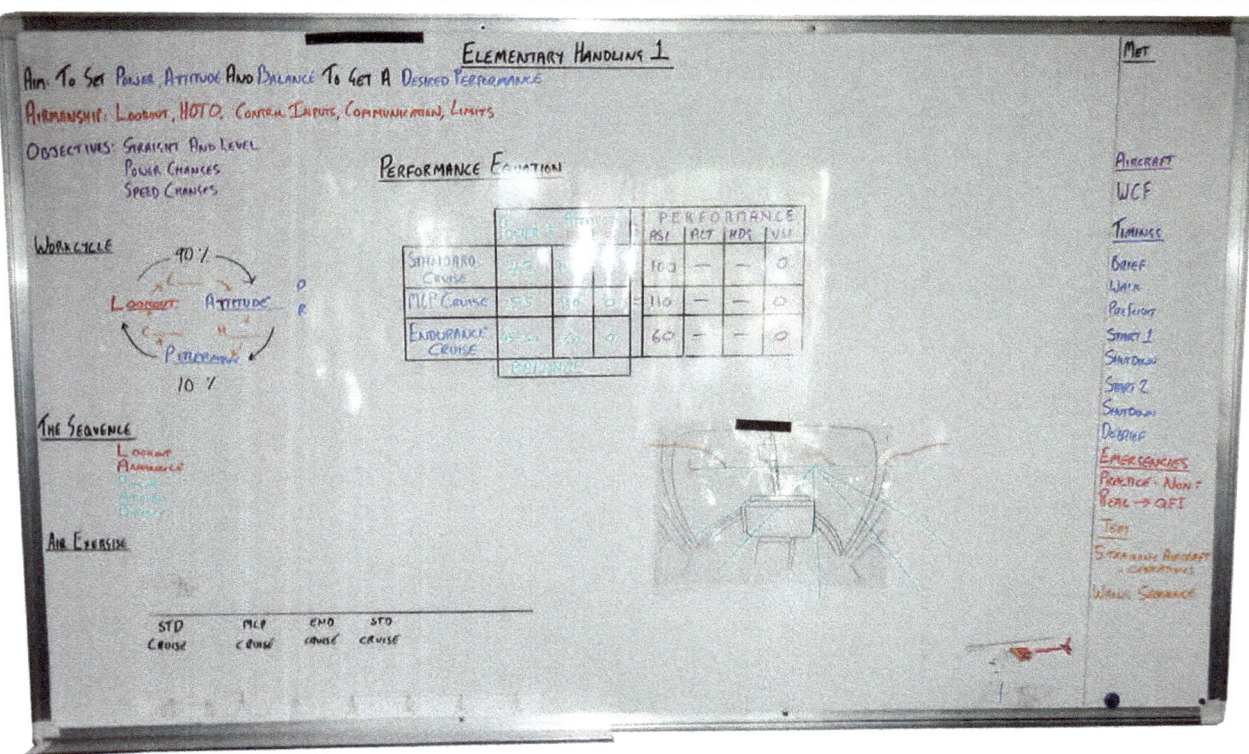

Mike Becker, Becker Helicopters

Models

A good representation of the helicopter in the form of a model is the single best training aid an instructor can utilise and should be a mandatory bare minimum item.

It allows the instructor to demonstrate and give the trainee a graphic visual representation of what the helicopter will be doing. Good use of a helicopter model is a key element in the teaching process.

Cutaways and parts

Although these can be expensive, the use of helicopter and engine parts, particularly if they have been cutaway to expose the inner workings, is an excellent tool for giving the trainee insight into the function and construction of the item being discussed.

A good cutaway is worth a thousand words.

Charts and Posters

Many charts and posters may be prepared by the instructor or purchased. These can be very effective if placed on classroom walls or even given to the trainee to take home and use.

For example:

The Bureau of Meteorology produces a coloured chart showing various cloud forms. The Bureau of Air Safety and Civil Aviation have numerous posters available related to flight safety matters. For example, posters showing the instrument console:

Page 67

Principles and Methods of Instruction *for Helicopter Pilots*

Graphic Presentations

Anything that can give the trainee a visual representation of what is being discussed is helpful. This may take the form of simple line drawings on the whiteboard or projected through the computer right through to photographs, statistics, graphs, charts animations etc.

Movement	Control Name	Primary Effect	Desired Performance	Secondary Effects	Instrument (Primary Effect)	Instrument (Desired Performance)	Cues
	Throttle (N2 Beep)	N1 Gas Producer RPM	N2 Turbine RPM	YAW (HDG) PITCH (ATT) Torque and TOT			
	Pedals	Yaw (Heading)	BALANCE (BAL)	POWER (Tq) ROLL (ATT) ALTITUDE (ALT)			
	Collective	Power (Tq)	ALTITUDE (ALT)	YAW (HDG) PITCH (ATT)			
	Cyclic	Pitch Attitude (Pitch)	IAS (ASI)	ALTITUDE (ALT) YAW (Heading)			
		Roll Attitude (Roll)	HEADING (DG/HSI/Compass)	ALTITUDE (ALT) ADVERSE YAW (BAL)			

Managing Training Aids

The most effective use of training aids involves some degree of stage management by the instructor for maximum impact.

Movement

The eye, and therefore trainees' attention, is naturally attracted to things that move, including gestures and body movement by the instructor. Pointing specifically to visual aids and the use of movable models can enhance a lesson's effectiveness.

Colour

The use of colour provides variety and interest and can convey relativity and reinforce concepts

For example:

- The use of red for important items such as Airmanship or Danger (be careful not to overuse Red, for example, don't just use it for emphasis).
- The use of black for general text.
- The use of blue or green for thrust or lift and the use of red for drag.

Synchronisation

Continuity should be maintained between the use of aids and the spoken word. The instructor should "talk over" the visual aid and not allow the aid to be the centre of attention.

Although instructors should strive to give their lessons impact (The Law of Effect), they should not forget that their primary responsibility is to teach and not necessarily to entertain, their trainees.

Many otherwise excellent instructors have become so involved with the use of aids that their trainees remember them more for their showmanship rather than the skills, knowledge and behaviours they were supposed to be learning.

Conclusion

Training aids are to be used to enhance the teaching process, not replace it.

They need to be used at the appropriate time to enhance a teaching point and give a visual representation of what the instructor is verbally describing.

Principles and Methods of Instruction *for Helicopter Pilots*

Appendices

Appendix A: PIRC Exam Competencies

The syllabus for the PMI exam will include the following items taken from CASR Part 61 Volume 3 Section 2.4.[14]

SECTION 2.4 INSTRUCTOR RATINGS

Unit 2.4.1 FIRC: Instructor rating – common (based on the 18 May 2021 release)

1.			Reserved
2.			**Flight Rules**
	2.1		**Legislation**
		2.1.1	Describe the privileges and limitations of the instructor rating and associated training endorsements
		2.1.2	Describe the flight training that must be conducted under the authority of Part 141 or 142 of CASR 1998
3.			**Principles and methods of instruction**
	3.1		**Principles of Learning**
		3.1.1	Describe the adult learning process.
		3.1.2	Explain what is meant by perception.
		3.1.3	Explain the relative importance of each of the physical senses in learning.
		3.1.4	Explain how the defence mechanisms listed may hinder learning: (a) rationalisation; (b) flight; (c) aggression; (d) resignation.
		3.1.5	Explain how the level of stress may affect learning.
		3.1.6	Explain the relation between perception and understanding.
		3.1.7	State how positive and negative motivation affects learning.
		3.1.8	Explain the application of the levels of learning.
		3.1.9	Explain how the rate of learning may vary with practice.
		3.1.10	Explain the role of each of the memory systems in terms of the model of information processing: (a) sensory register; (b) short-term memory; (c) long term memory.
	3.2		**Principles of Instruction**
		3.2.1	Explain how a flight instructor could assist the process of perception and understanding.
		3.2.3	State examples of how rote learning, understanding of knowledge and correlation apply to flight training.

---

[14] https://www.legislation.gov.au/Details/F2021C00449/Html/Volume_3" \l "_Toc395460952

3.2.3 Identify the outcomes of aeronautical knowledge instruction associated with the 3 domains of learning:
(a) cognitive (knowledge);
(b) affective (attitudes, beliefs and values);
(c) psychomotor (physical skills).

3.2.4 State the factors that may hinder learning with respect to aeronautical knowledge training.

3.2.5 Explain the advantages and disadvantages of guided discussion in flight training and identify flight training activities for which this technique could be suitable.

3.2.6 Give examples of positive and negative transfer in aeronautical knowledge training.

3.2.7 Explain the role of each factor listed in the communication process:
(a) source;
(b) symbols;
(c) receiver.

3.2.8 Recall how these common barriers affect communication:
(a) lack of common experience;
(b) confusion;
(c) abstractions.

3.2.9 Explain how an instructor may monitor, whether communication has been achieved.

3.2.10 Identify adult learning issues applicable to aeronautical knowledge training.

3.2.11 Explain each of the basic steps of the teaching process:
(a) preparation;
(b) presentation;
(c) application;
(d) review and evaluation.

3.2.12 State the purpose of behavioural (performance-based) outcomes in flight training.

3.2.13 Explain the following attributes of effective outcomes:
(a) achievable;
(b) observable;
(c) measurable.

3.2.14 Explain how to develop the 3 essential elements of behavioural outcomes:
(a) performance (what has to be done);
(b) performance criteria;
(c) conditions.

3.2.15 Explain the advantages and disadvantages of the teaching methods listed and give practical examples of situations best suited to each of these techniques in flight training:
(a) lecture;
(b) theory or skill lesson;
(c) group learning;
(d) guided discussion;
(e) briefing.

Principles and Methods of Instruction *for Helicopter Pilots*

	3.2.16	Explain the role of the instructor in each of the 5 steps involved in providing skill practice to trainees: (a) explanation; (b) demonstration; (c) performance; (d) supervision; (e) evaluation.
	3.2.17	Explain the difference between a training syllabus and competency-based standards.
3.3		**Lesson planning and delivery**
	3.3.1	Explain the general purpose and content of each of the components of a typical aeronautical knowledge lesson plan: (a) aim/motivation/revision; (b) outcomes; (c) explanation of principles; (d) explanation/demonstration of technique; (e) threat and error management; (f) practice; (g) review.
	3.3.2	State the reasons for limiting the duration of lessons and indicate the desirable duration of a typical lesson.
	3.3.3	Explain the purpose and content of a training syllabus (or curriculum).
	3.3.4	Explain the purpose and use of training aids.
	3.3.5	Give examples of training aids particularly suited to aeronautical knowledge training.
	3.3.6	Explain the role of the instructor in each of the following phases of review and evaluation: (a) fault analysis (diagnosis); (b) competency assessment; (c) trainee self-assessment; (d) training effectiveness.
3.4		**Principles of Questioning**
	3.4.1	Explain the reasons for questioning trainees.
	3.4.2	Explain the characteristics of an effective or open question.
	3.4.3	Give examples of good and poor questions.
	3.4.4	Explain how oral questions can promote mental activity.
	3.4.5	Explain why oral questions maintain student interest during a lesson.
	3.4.6	Explain why is it essential that the instructor always confirm answers to questions.
	3.4.7	Explain the purposes of oral questions.
	3.4.8	Describe the desired qualities of good oral questions.
	3.4.9	Describe the procedure to follow when asking a question.
	3.4.10	Explain the key points to observe in the handling of student answers.
	3.4.11	Explain the key points to observe in the handling of student questions.

Appendix B: Example Lesson Plan - Elementary Handling 1

Aim

To develop the work cycle and use the performance equation, as well as knowledge of the effects of controls, to achieve straight and level flight at varying speeds: Namely: Standard Cruise, Endurance Cruise and MCP Cruise.

Duration

Sortie Time: 1.2

Ground Time: 0.5

Resources Required

- Aircraft: B206BIII (standard configuration)
- Maps and Charts: ERSA, VTC

Trainee preparation

- Review RFM and technical notes for the aircraft.
- Practice listening and noting down ATIS for the next sortie.
- Review Pilot Handling Notes for Elementary Handling.
- Revisit work cycle and practice dry flying it.
- Review Hung start emergency procedure for next sortie.
- Review Engine hot shutdown emergency procedure for next sortie.
- Review procedure for CAUT or WNG LT illumination for next sortie.

Prerequisites

BAS-03 EOC in Forward Flight.

Training Areas and Limitations

- Class G airspace. An open, unpopulated area.
- Met conditions: Easily visible horizon, Cloud base as high as possible

Aircrew Configuration

Multi-crew, with Instructor as PIC.

Instructor demonstrates and directs trainee, following the Handover and Takeover Procedure.

Standards

- Manual Of Standards Assessment Standards Part 61 Manual of Standards – Elementary Handling
- Pilot Handling Notes, Chapter 5 – Elementary Handling
- Accuracy holding power and attitude Standard:
    - Airspeeds plus or minus **15 KIAS**
    - Altitudes plus or minus **500 ft**
    - Heading plus or minus **30 deg**
    - Power plus or minus **10% TQ**.
- Demonstration standards:
    - Smooth controlled inputs (rate and magnitude)
    - Correct coordination of controls
    - Correct order of controls (power attitude balance)

Principles and Methods of Instruction *for Helicopter Pilots*

Objectives

- Develop the work cycle and apply performance equation.
- Able to recall and understand the effects of all the primary flight controls to achieve straight and level flight at varied speeds.
- Developing the knowledge and control to be able to perform and maintain a:
    - Standard cruise
    - Endurance cruise
    - MCP cruise
- Developing the knowledge and control to be able to make configuration changes.
- Able to maintain airspeeds plus or minus 15 KIAS, Altitudes plus or minus 500 ft, heading plus or minus 30 deg, plus or minus 10%TQ.

Briefing And Planning

Long Brief

- BAS-04-BRF – Elementary Handling

Presentations and other resources

- BAS-04-PRS – Elementary Handling

Discussion Points

- Correct pre-start actions up to engine start.
- Working application of the 'work cycle'.
- Correct verbalisation of 'work cycle' when directed.

Common Faults

- The trainee struggles to locate a reference point inside to align with the horizon.
- The trainee fixates on the reference point and its alignment to the horizon but fails to keep the horizon flat which turns the aircraft.
- The trainee over controls the aircraft with harsh inputs causing him to continually chase the horizon with the ref point.
- The trainee fails to react to the aircraft attitude moving away from the horizon.
- The trainee fails to conduct the work cycle.
- The trainee fixates on the instruments, including the AI, and tries to chase performance without setting attitude.
- The trainee struggles to use three controls together and flies out of balance or allows the collective to drop causing unwanted yaw and pitch down of the nose resulting in incorrect attitude.
- The trainee fails to select a reference point on the horizon to fly towards causing the aircraft to wander around the sky.
- The trainee doesn't have a full understanding of the performance equation resulting in a poor understanding of the necessity to maintain a consistent power and attitude to give a performance.

Sortie Plan

Activity	Action
Crew mission pre-flight brief	- Participate in crew mission pre-flight brief. - Must be on time, with notebook and pen and any notes relating to the brief without guidance.

Pre-flight brief questions	- Is able to answer 75% of these questions:
	    - State the work cycle, its key elements, and how attention is divided (%) as one uses it.
	    - Define Attitude flying (how does he maintain pitch and roll).
	    - State the Performance equation.
	    - State the sequence of control configuration adjustments when changing from Standard cruise to Endurance Cruise.

Activity	Action
Conduct aircraft pre-flight inspection	<ul><li>Conduct pre-flight as per checklist.</li><li>Demonstrate aircraft technical knowledge<ul><li>Ask trainee to identify and explain the purpose of the vertical stabiliser.</li><li>Discuss the effect of varied airspeed on balance.</li></ul></li></ul>
Conduct start checks	<ul><li>Confirm that the trainee sits correctly</li><li>Adjusts his pedals and harness correctly</li><li>Sets kneeboard and maps correctly</li><li>Takes down the ATIS</li><li>Direct/monitor pre-start checks as per checklist</li><li>Emergency consolidation</li><li>Discuss: Hung start emergency</li><li>Direct/monitor start checks as per checklist</li><li>Direct/monitor run up checks as per checklist</li></ul>
Conduct correct radio procedures	Monitor:<ul><li>Turn on, correctly tune radio and listen to ATIS.</li></ul>
Perform pre lift off checks	<ul><li>Direct and Monitor as per the checklist.</li><li>**Note:**<ul><li>Ensure the aircraft is in correct configuration before handing over.</li><li>Correct demonstrations are imperative – if the demonstration is inaccurate, - stop, -do it again.</li><li>Remember at this stage one of the best ways the trainee is learning is by the 'monkey see – monkey do' principle, where the trainee will both consciously and sub-consciously emulate your behaviours.</li></ul></li></ul>
Perform airfield departure procedures	<ul><li>Demonstrate Lift off, Taxi, Take off</li></ul>
Revision	<ul><li>Review the effects of controls from previous sortie with emphasis on control inputs and secondary effects.</li><li>Highlight the main reasons for co-ordinating pedal and cyclic with power changes, and balance with speed and power changes.</li><li>Revise the need to LOOK out at the reference point and attitude during power and attitude changes.</li><li>Discuss and identify major reference features (for example, mountains and towns) in the local area.</li></ul>
Standard Cruise	<ul><li>DDM standard S+L cruise (75%TQ @ 100 kts)</li><li>Direct and Monitor standard S+L cruise (75% TQ @ 100 kts)</li><li>Get the trainee to remember with his thumb, where 75% is against his leg</li></ul>
Endurance Cruise	<ul><li>DDM endurance cruise (45 – 50 %TQ @ 60 kts)<ul><li>Note the correct order to decelerate: power attitude balance</li><li>Highlight the control inputs required to prevent the acft descending</li><li>Highlight the new reference point / attitude</li></ul></li></ul>
MCP cruise	<ul><li>DDM MCP cruise (85% TQ @ 110 kts)<ul><li>Note the correct order to accelerate: power attitude balance</li><li>Note control inputs required to prevent climbing</li><li>Highlight new reference point / attitude</li></ul></li></ul>

Activity	Action
Acceleration and Deceleration	- DM trainee practising acceleration and deceleration.
Climbs and Descents	- Demonstrate std climb and std descent - Note the same order of power, attitude, and balance. - Note attitudes especially that the act of maintaining an attitude can take considerable cyclic application
Return to base	- Demonstrate standard VMC approach (5-6 deg) - Demonstrate pre-landing checks, landing, after landing checks
Shutdown checks	- Monitor as per the checklist - Emergency consolidation - Flight: Perform engine hot shutdown emergency procedure

Post shutdown checks	- Direct post-flight aircraft checks as per checklist
	- Ensure trainee
	   - Leaves harnesses correctly
	   - Secures hatches and blades
	   - Carries out post-flight inspection
	   - Covers instruments and cockpit if applicable

Debrief	- Discuss:
	   - Sequence to change performance (PWR, ATT, BAL)
	   - Delay in turbine response
	   - Airmanship / lookout

Revision And Self Study

- Review Pilot Handling Notes for Elementary Handling
- Revise EOC in Forward Flight long brief
- Practice dry-flying (flying a chair) for previously learned sequences
- Study aircraft dimensions and limits.
- Review Hot start emergency procedure for next sortie.

References

Bibliography

- *Flying Instructors Handbook* (Central Flying School Australian Defence Force)
- *Personality Plus* (Florence Liteaur)
- *Helicopter Flying Handbook* (FAA)[15]
- *Aviation Instructor's Handbook* (FAA)[16]
- *Mind Tools: Theory X and Theory Y; Understanding Team Member Motivation*[17].
- *Wikipedia: Theory X and Theory Y*[18].
- *Businessballs.com: Douglas McGregor – Theory x y*[19]
- *Mind Tools: Herzberg's Motivators and Hygiene Factors: Learn How to Motivate Your Team*[20]
- *Wikipedia: Two-factor Theory*[21]
- *Businessballs.com: Frederick Herzberg Motivational Theory*[22]
- *Education Portal: Frederick Herzberg Theory of Motivation*[23]

Attribution for images

Chetan, V. (2019). *Low Angle Photography of Man Jumping (cropped)*. Pexels.Com. https://www.pexels.com/photo/low-angle-photography-of-man-jumping-2923156/

Draper, E. (2003). *George W. Bush's official portrait, 2003*. https://en.wikipedia.org/wiki/George_W._Bush#/media/File:George-W-Bush.jpeg

McNeely, B. (1993). *Bill Clinton's official portrait, 1993*. https://en.wikipedia.org/wiki/Bill_Clinton#/media/File:Bill_Clinton.jpg

NAA. (n.d.-a). *About Gough Whitlam*. Retrieved June 16, 2021, from https://www.naa.gov.au/explore-collection/australias-prime-ministers/gough-whitlam

NAA. (n.d.-b). *About Kevin Rudd*. Retrieved June 16, 2021, from https://www.naa.gov.au/explore-collection/australias-prime-ministers/kevin-rudd

Portrait of PM John Winston Howard. Circa 2001. (2006). https://en.wikipedia.org/wiki/John_Howard#/media/File:Howard_John_BANNER.jpg

Portrait of PM Robert James Lee Hawke. Date unknown. (2006). https://en.wikipedia.org/wiki/Bob_Hawke#/media/File:Hawke_Bob_BANNER.jpg

RODNAE Productions. (2020). *Man in Black Long Sleeve Shirt Sitting on Brown Wooden Chair (cropped)*. Pexels.Com. https://www.pexels.com/photo/menu-restaurant-man-people-4921084/

Souza, P. (2012). *Obama standing with his arms folded and smiling*. https://en.wikipedia.org/wiki/Barack_Obama#/media/File:President_Barack_Obama.jpg

---

[15] https://www.faa.gov/regulations_policies/handbocks_manuals/aviation/helicopter_flying_handbook/

[16] https://www.faa.gov/regulations_policies/handbocks_manuals/aviation/aviation_instructors_handbook/

[17] http://www.mindtools.com/pages/article/newLDR_74.htm

[18] http://en.wikipedia.org/wiki/Theory_X_and_Theory_Y

[19] http://www.businessballs.com/mcgregor.htm

[20] http://www.mindtools.com/pages/article/newTMM_74.htm

[21] http://en.wikipedia.org/wiki/Two-factor_theory

[22] http://www.businessballs.com/herzberg.htm

[23] http://education-portal.com/academy/lesson/frederick-herzbergs-theory-of-motivation-lesson-quiz.html#lesson

Abbreviations

The following abbreviations are used in this manual.

Abbreviation	Title
PMI	Principles and Methods of Instruction
FIR	Flight Instructor Rating
TE	Training Endorsement
CASA	Civil Aviation Safety Authority of Australia
CASR	Civil Aviation Safety Regulations
PIRC	Pilot Instructor Rating Common (PIRC) examination
FAA	Federal Aviation Administration, the US aviation regulator.